*Creating Your Future:*
*A Guide to Personal Goal Setting*

# Creating Your Future:
# A Guide to Personal Goal Setting

**George A. Ford**
**Gordon L. Lippitt**

**Revised by George A. Ford**

**University Associates, Inc.**
**8517 Production Avenue**
**San Diego, California 92121**

Copyright © 1988 by University Associates, Inc.
ISBN: 0-88390-221-4
Library of Congress Catalog Card Number: 88-50619
Printed in the United States of America

Expanded and revised from the previously published
*Planning Your Future: A Workbook for Personal Goal Setting*

*Senior Editor & Book Designer: Carol Nolde*

*Cover Designer: Janet Colby*

# Dedicated to
# Gordon L. Lippitt (1920-1985)

It has been exceptionally difficult to revise and update this little book, and it took me months to realize why. It certainly was not a lack of new material; the technology of career and life planning has improved immensely in the last twelve years. It was because I missed one of Gordon L. Lippitt's many, many talents: his amazing ability to come up with the right word or phrase when I felt stuck. I would call him and say, "Gordon, I can't get this blankety-blank paragraph right. Why did I agree to do all this work anyway?" Gordon would let me ramble for a while, then laughingly come up with four or five ideas that would get me back on track. I miss him, and I know many of our colleagues miss him. Although I have tried hard to make this workbook interesting and useful for the reader, his touch will be missed here, too.

In the course of our lifetimes, Gordon and I did not have a lot of contact—probably not even a month's time, including meetings, seminars, workshops, telephone calls, classes, correspondence, and work sessions on this book. But his optimism, his upbeat approach to life, his caring contact with others, his efforts to practice what he preached, and his ability to plan and solve problems spontaneously left a lasting impression. If there were some way to package some of Gordon's qualities in this edition of *Creating Your Future*, this workbook would be a treasured gift for any reader.

Since this is a dedication, I'm going to indulge in some stories about Gordon that exemplify his approach to planning his future. When I met Gordon in 1968, he was making a transition from his career as president of a publishing company to another of his many careers. The last time I saw him in 1985, when George Washington University threw a day-and-a-half-long celebration in honor of his retirement, he was talking about slowing down some after revising this workbook and completing several other projects. We talked about using some newer technology and putting this workbook on videotape or audiotape.

He was future oriented, yet grounded in the present. Watching him function in a meeting was like seeing a textbook in group dynamics in action. He listened hard and always seemed to be able to be constructive. At one meeting Gordon seemed to be doodling, but actually he was sketching a picture of who was speaking to whom. The status person in the meeting, Tom, seemed to be blocking all attempts at progress until Gordon started speaking directly to Tom with arguments in favor of what the other group members had agreed on. The members then came to quick agreement and moved ahead. Later, when asked about this approach, Gordon explained that from his diagraming he had figured out that Tom was not listening to anyone but him; consequently, he began to speak for the group. Tom listened, and the group was able to proceed. Gordon was practicing what he frequently taught others.

In the mid-Seventies I took a leadership course that Gordon taught. There were only about ten graduate students, and we met informally in Gordon's office. During each class after the first, a student would make a presentation for about a half-hour; then the group would spend the next hour and a half in an often-heated and always-exciting discussion. Gordon was an active participant/leader in the discussions, and I can quote many of his comments even today. I learned an enormous amount, and I believe that the other students did too. Amazingly, Gordon seemed to learn as much as, or more than, the rest of us. Even when the content was not new to him, he saw an opportunity to relearn or to look at things from a new angle. It is Gordon Lippitt's kind of attitude toward learning that assures a future full of satisfactions.

Gordon, thousands of us learned an awful lot from you.

George A. Ford
April, 1988

# *Preface*

This edition is actually the third revision of a work that started while I was a participant in The NTL Institute for Applied Behavioral Science's "Program for Specialists in Organization Development" in August, 1968. The first edition was published in 1972, after I met Gordon Lippitt, who both inspired me to complete it and helped write it. At that time it was called *A Life Planning Workbook*. In retrospect it was a primitive version of today's life-planning technology. We created a tool for people who could not or did not want to participate with others in a course or workshop; they completed the workbook on their own and were able to focus their energies on things that were important to them.

The Revised Edition, published in 1976, was initiated because the original publisher was running out of copies of the first edition. With the reprinting University Associates wanted to retitle the book as *Planning Your Future*. Gordon and I added all of the new planning tools that space would allow in appendixes, but retained the basic format of three planning sessions.

Two developments served as the impetus for the present revision:

1. Great improvement in the methods and techniques available to help people take more control over their lives; and

2. The realization that people were not only using the book alone, but were creating partnerships or were using the book as a text in workshops to complete the planning activities.

Consequently, the book has been updated to be more useful as a group guide. Also, because it now includes so many more tools to help people focus and create satisfactions for themselves, there are now five work sessions.

Gordon Lippitt's death in 1985 was a powerful reminder to me of how our world has changed in the years since the first edition was published. Many such changes had happened in our own lives: Gordon had retired from teaching and changed his career; I had moved through four internal, consulting-manager assignments for the old Bell System in four different cities before eventually taking a sabbatical and developing an independent consulting practice. Gordon's death was also a sad lesson in how fragile our existence is. I know Gordon would say that such an event only points out the importance of planning, focusing energy on what you want to do, and creating more of your own "kicks" in life.

Change continues, of course, and is no longer much of a surprise to anyone. The dilemma is how to describe changes rather than how to accept them. I recently asked eleven senior behavioral-science colleagues, who belong to an informal professional support group called the Phrogs, to help me describe the changes in the past fifteen years. We read the Preface to the 1976 edition of this book as well as the Introduction to the 1972 edition (both of which follow this preface) and then brainstormed a list of changes. The translation, interpretation, additions to, deletions from, and articulation of the list are entirely my responsibility; but I thank my fellow Phrogs for their ideas:

- In 1976 we were using the term "the post-industrial society" because we did not yet have a name for what we now call "the information age."

- Inflation in much of the world has been under control for a few years now, and the outlook is for the continuation of inflation levels well below double digits as long as there is an oversupply of oil.

- The impact of international events on our lives is more evident and more understood. Wars, terrorism, and dollar devaluations are educating us about our economic and other ties to people all over the world. The imminence of manufacturing in space adds another dimension.

- The mental set of "one job for life" or "one company for life," which was prevalent before the 1970s, was altered with the massive downsizing and layoffs that occurred in our largest organizations. Now more jobs are being created by small, new companies than by the Fortune 500 giants. The inability of major organizations, which are faced with rapid change, to guarantee lifetime employment has created the acceptance of multiple careers and all of the stress generated by changing jobs.

- Minority groups' search for power has evolved into demands for equity. This development reflects not only growing power but also growing frustration with conservative administrations that are seen as de-emphasizing the thrust toward greater equity for all.

- Fears created by AIDS have caused a major shift in the sexual revolution. There is growing evidence that the incidence of intercourse with multiple partners is decreasing. Certainly the media deal in more explicit presentations about sexual practices, and so does the Surgeon General of the United States.

- Videocassette recorders have brought more and better entertainment and education options into the home, work place, and classroom. Large segments of the population have seen themselves on TV and are documenting their lives on videotape. With the availability of sexually explicit videos, one might speculate that changes in sexual habits have been influenced by these videos.

- Other health issues are also becoming prominent. The assault on heart disease is apparent in widely visible efforts to reduce the salt, caffeine, saturated fat, and cholesterol in our western diets. In addition, the importance of exercise is being emphasized in many areas.

- As more and more work becomes automated, the possibility arises that someday the only work left for people will be to learn and to care for one another.

- Our aging populations have started to become more visible. For example, seniors are seen behind the counters in fast-food restaurants. This development reminds us that Social Security and other old-age support systems will become strained when there are more people relying on these systems than there are people working. It also points out that people need to plan and make decisions carefully so that they can spend their later years in satisfying ways.

- The quest for satisfaction in the work place (quality of work life) has become a part of the overall quest for improved quality of life.

- Hope for the avoidance of a nuclear war is being generated by the expectation of a missile treaty between the United States and Russia in 1988.

The increased complexity of our lives means that more decisions have to be made and more personal stress is created—more reasons for us to be grounded in who we are, what we believe in, and what we want.

This edition is over twice as large as the last. New features include the following:

1. An activity on creating a vision statement of your future;

2. Information on risk taking;

3. New material on individual power and positive ways to use it to meet your needs;

4. A new section on modifying and/or creating your job or career (including activities on identifying satisfiers and dissatisfiers at work and devising a job action plan for deriving greater satisfaction from your current job as well as focusing on what you want from your next job);

5. A new section on identifying, clarifying, and prioritizing values (including two activities based on the contributions of Donald H. Bullock: an evaluation of twenty-two "areas" of life and an assessment of the relative importance of these "areas" or values);

6. A new appendix that presents an easy way of contracting with others to help you accomplish what you want to accomplish; and

7. Many new sample workbook responses (people's real contributions) to coincide with new activities.

An important feature of this edition is its emphasis on your own power to create the future you want. M. Scott Peck, in his book *The Road Less Traveled* (published by Simon & Schuster in 1985), eloquently makes the point that although life is difficult, once you accept this fact you can stop wasting energy worrying about it and feeling sorry for yourself. It is difficult for everyone everywhere, but those who have found a way to use goals and objectives to their benefit discover that the pain of living is hardly noticeable if you have your eye on something you want. I hope this book will help you focus on and create a future that is particularly satisfying to you.

April, 1988

George A. Ford
Annapolis, Maryland

# *Preface to the 1976 Edition*

As our society moves from being basically an industrial society to one with the new values, norms, and behavior of a post-industrial world, many people are experiencing the need to reorganize their goals and reshape their lives.

Four years ago we finished our work on the first edition of this workbook. Since then, the world has continued its kaleidoscopic alteration in conditions around us and in many of the attitudes that go with them. A combination of forces has triggered:

- Worldwide inflation causing widespread unemployment and, for the first time in our adult lives, a reduction in real income;
- A wider gap between the powerful and rich and the powerless and poor;
- Continued changes in value systems;
- People's greater expectations of services;
- The expanded influence of governments;
- An increased desire for power by minority groups;
- A continued rise in the influence of mass media;
- The extensive and progressive evolution of education as it applies to continued growth and development at all ages;
- A shift from a production to a service economy;
- A continued expansion of technology;
- The emergence of new avocations and vocations in society;
- Greater international interdependence;
- Persisting ecological concerns;
- More mobility of people with less commitment to an organization or community;
- A growth in the size of the social systems of mankind resulting in a greater feeling of powerlessness in members of such systems;
- A continued explosion of knowledge; and
- A desire for quality, not just quantity, as a goal of life.

These trends are accelerating at an uneven rate, but at a speed that challenges all our institutions, as well as the individual who works within them. The total picture describes a transition from the industrial to the post-industrial society and massive changes that are not under control, a dilemma well stated by Eric Trist:

*The contemporary environment...is taking on the quality of a turbulent field.... This turbulence grossly increases the area of relative uncertainty for individuals and organizations alike. It raises far-reaching problems concerning the limits of human adaptation. Forms of adaptation, both personal and organizational, developed to meet a simpler type of environment, no longer suffice to meet the higher levels of complexity now coming into existence.... The planner's dilemma...may be summarized as follows: the greater the degree of change, the greater the need for planning—otherwise precedents of the past could guide the future; but the greater the degree of uncertainty, the greater the likelihood that plans right today will be wrong tomorrow. (p. 29)[1]*

With all the change and confusion around us, we feel grateful that we have been fortunate enough to learn some skills in life planning that give us a fairly stable base and the confidence that we are still in control of our own lives. The revisions in this edition represent new learnings for us that we would like to share with others.

The new additions are:

- A section on making decisions that should build the confidence of those wanting to try life planning;

- A section on Family Life Cycle and Needs;

- An appendix section for organizations that are considering providing life planning assistance for their members (this includes a check list to help determine if such assistance would support the organization's needs and goals);

- A Force-Field Analysis Inventory;

- A bibliography of recommended readings for those who wish to read further.

Coping with one's life involves coping with change and stability. We hope that the process in this workbook will contribute to both and at the same time be challenging, fun, helpful, and revealing.

We gratefully acknowledge the contributions of Herbert Shepard and Arthur Shedlin through their pioneer work in the field of life planning.

April, 1976

George A. Ford
Baltimore, Maryland

Gordon L. Lippitt
Washington, D.C.

---

[1]From "Between Cultures: The Current Crisis of Transition" by E. Trist, 1970, in *Organizational Frontiers and Human Values* by W. Schmidt (Ed.), Belmont, CA: Wadsworth. Reprinted by permission.

# *Introduction to the 1972 Edition*

As our society moves from being basically an industrial society to the new values, norms, and behavior of a post-industrial world, many people are experiencing the need to reorganize their goals and reshape their lives. As two persons who have developed new career paths on several occasions, we wanted to share a process to help people examine their life goals and plans. Coping with one's life involves both change and stability. We hope that the process in this workbook will contribute to both. We feel that this venture can be challenging, fun, helpful, and revealing.

We gratefully acknowledge the contributions of Herbert Shepard and Arthur Shedlin for their pioneer work in the field of life planning.

1972

George Ford
Gordon Lippitt

# Contents

*. . .the best way to predict the future is to invent it.*

John Sculley & John A. Byrne, 1987
*Odyssey: Pepsi to Apple*, p. 297

# 1

# *Guidelines for Planned Personal Growth*

The following guidelines about personal growth may be helpful as you work your way through this book:

- Personal goal setting is a process of systematically growing as a person while accomplishing specific purposes in your life.

- Personal growth involves changes in attitudes and behaviors that are related to your self-concept and your needs.

- Personal growth may not be possible in all areas of your life. Heredity or strong early environmental forces may hinder even desirable changes. This fact need not be demotivating, though; it simply means that you should not put unrealistic demands on yourself. To do so would divert your energies from those goals that you *can* realistically accomplish.

- If you have certain habits, attitudes, and opinions that reduce your receptiveness to alternative ways of thinking and acting, they may keep you from changing and growing in the ways you would like. Keep an open mind as you work through the process of creating your future; try not to be limited by the boundaries of your current situation.

- If you have defensive behavior patterns, they may deter your change and growth by providing mechanisms for distorting reality.

- Personal growth may be accelerated by attitudes and behaviors that are marked by openness, receptivity to new experiences, curiosity, risk taking, eagerness, lack of fear, and experimentation.

- We human beings are incredibly complex; we differ in our degrees of self-understanding as well as our levels and kinds of aspirations. Nevertheless, most of us desire some kind of personal growth.

- Generally we tend to underestimate our abilities and our potential for accomplishment and personal growth.

This workbook provides a simple structure for creating your future through personal growth and development. It is a step-by-step process that enables you to accomplish the following:

1. Develop a written record of a number of dimensions of your personality;

2. Discover which areas of your work provide you with the greatest satisfaction/dissatisfaction;

3. Recognize, reaffirm, and set priorities for the broad goals that you have at this point in your life;

4. Clarify which of your aspirations and values you should focus on and which you should put aside; and

5. Develop a project that combines several of your future priority goals, values, and desires.

One final—and very important—point: Your future belongs to you; you have control over it. You can take responsibility for what your life will be, design it, orchestrate it, and turn your goals into reality; or you can let other people or external events dictate what your life will be. Creating your own future involves working hard and taking some risks; it means being *proactive* instead of *reactive*. But it can also yield great returns and the satisfaction of knowing that what you have created is truly yours. As Peter Block (1987, p. 189) says:

*The challenge is to pursue our vision*
*with as much courage and intensity*
*as we can generate.*

## REFERENCE

Block, P. (1987). *The empowered manager: Positive political skills at work*. San Francisco: Jossey-Bass.

# How to Use This Workbook

Although this workbook is designed for individual use, you will derive the greatest benefit from it if you work through it with one or more partners. For example, families, couples, and co-workers with a commitment to developing teamwork can use this approach. It is possible to complete it by yourself, but if you do so you will lose an important advantage. A great deal of data on life and career planning suggests that the planning process is much more useful when completed with other people. There is a lot to be said for bouncing ideas off another person whom you trust and whose perceptions and opinions you respect. If you do choose to work with one or more others, each of you will need a separate workbook.

Throughout this workbook you will find boxed notes addressed to the reader who is working with one or more partners. These notes ask the reader to stop and share thoughts or just-completed work with his or her partner(s). If you are working with others, follow the instructions given in the notes; if you are working alone, ignore these notes when you see them. The following is an example of such a note:

---

**Note: Share the work you just completed with your partner(s).**

---

Here are some suggestions for completing the process presented in the workbook:

1. *Work through the planning sessions and complete the tasks in the order in which they are presented.* Don't skip ahead! The planning process is an integrated one that is designed to help you understand yourself and create your future more effectively. If you have patience and persistence in working step by step until you have completed the process, you will be pleased with the results of your work.

2. *Be aware that there are no incorrect responses to any tasks or questions in this workbook.* The tasks are designed to help you bring out information about yourself on paper so that you can organize it, use it, share it with others, and remember it more easily. All your answers will be right for you, just as other people's answers will be right for them.

3. *Write in pencil in the workbook to encourage yourself to change whatever you want to change.* You should feel free to rework your ideas, specify them, correct them, add to them, or delete them. The planning process involves continually clarifying the future that you want.

4. *Write your own responses before consulting with your partner(s) or referring to the appendixes.* At various points you will be instructed to write your thoughts and to compare them with those of your partners, if you are working with others, and with those in Appendix A, which were written by people who worked on similar tasks. As a result of your comparisons, you will find that some comments will "ring a bell" for you and you will say, "Yes, that's the way I feel, too." However, you will also reject some comments: "I'm not that way at all." The purpose of the comparisons is to provide you with illustrations of the variety of ways in which people reflect on their lives and to help you clarify information about yourself. Avoid the trap of patterning your responses after those of others or using other people's responses to evaluate your own. In creating your future, your own thoughts are valid for you in a way that no one else's can be.

5. *After you have worked through a session, wait one to four days before proceeding to the next one.* Each of the five sessions presented in the workbook is intended to be completed in a single planning period. The length of each planning period is entirely up to you. Of course, if you are working alone, you can spend as long as you like. If you are working with one partner, the minimum time required is about two hours; but you may find that you need quite a bit more time, depending on how many partners you have, how long you and your partner(s) spend discussing various issues, and so on.

6. *Complete the sessions in a place where you feel comfortable and where you will be free from interruptions.* Treat the creation of your future as the important and valuable task that it is; give it your undivided attention.

# *First Planning Session*

## *DRAWING YOUR LIFELINE*

Throughout our lives, all of us have been setting goals or objectives and striving to accomplish them. Some of these goals are conscious and clearly defined, but many are below our level of awareness. The one-year-old's striving to walk and the ninety-year-old's striving to live to see the sun rise another day are examples of human goals at the extreme ends of the continuum of life. Our goals or expectations—conscious or unconscious—determine our actions. To focus your thinking for the task of goal setting, complete a simple diagram for yourself according to the following instructions. (Resist the temptation to read and not write. The experience of putting pencil to paper is important.)

Think creatively

1. Let the left edge of this page represent the beginning of your life and the right edge of the page represent the end of your life. Start at the left edge and draw the line all the way to the right edge, going up or down to represent important stages and/or events in your life. Consider not only your past and present but also your future.

2. After you have drawn the line, place a check mark (✔) to indicate where you are now.

Now that you have a graphic representation of the aspects of your life that you consciously and subconsciously considered when you drew the line, write a few brief statements to complete the following items:

*1. I drew the line in this way because...*

*2. I put the check mark where I did because...*

Note: Share the work you just completed with your partner(s).

Next turn to Appendix A, "1. Lifelines", and compare your lines with those drawn by other people.

Note: Share your thoughts on the examples with your partner(s).

After making comparisons, what have you discovered about yourself? Write your responses in the following spaces. (Example: *I'm a unique individual, different in many ways from others who drew lifelines but similar in some ways.*)

1.

2.

3.

4.

| Note: Share the work you just completed with your partner(s). |

## CREATING YOUR VISION

In the rest of this session, you will be devising goals and objectives for yourself. First, though, you need to formulate a *life vision*—a general statement of the future as you *want* it to be, not as you predict it might be. While working on your vision, try to suspend your internal critic as well as any inclination to be modest or prudent. At this point don't concern yourself with whether your vision is achievable. This is a time to entertain notions of greatness, to reach as far as your desires will take you. In his book *Odyssey: Pepsi to Apple* (Sculley & Byrne, 1987, p. 3), John Sculley, former president of Pepsi-Cola, describes the moment when he learned that Pepsi was number one and had at last outperformed Coke: "We always believed, since the early seventies, when Pepsi was widely viewed as the perennial also-ran, that we could do it. All of us started out with that objective, and we never took our eyes off it." The objective he talks about is the *vision* he had for Pepsi-Cola. Your vision should be just as inspiring.

Keep in mind that your vision will lay the foundation for your future and for all of your goals and objectives; therefore, *you must be willing to commit to your vision.* The rest of the planning that you do in this workbook must be consistent with—and will be tested against—your vision statement. By recording your vision and committing yourself to it, you make yourself accountable for your future actions.

Once you decide what your vision is, record it in the following space. Because your objective is to state the future you want in *general* terms, be brief; write no more than three or four sentences. You will deal with specifics later.

*My vision of my future:*

Now ask yourself the following questions:

1. Does this vision stretch me as a person?

2. Does it inspire me?

3. Am I willing to commit to it?

4. Am I willing to test it against all of my future goals, objectives, and actions?

If the answer to any of these questions is "no," rework your vision statement until you can answer "yes" to every question.

After you have finished working on your vision statement, turn to Appendix A, "2. Vision Statements," and review the life visions of others.

## A WORD ABOUT GOALS AND OBJECTIVES

The dictionary defines the words *goal* and *objective* similarly. In this workbook the two words will be used interchangeably as "something desirable; something to be achieved; an expectation; an end to be reached; a target to strive for or to aim at." A personal goal is something that you want to obtain or maintain and that you are willing to take action to achieve. Both *desire* and *willingness to act* must be present.

Goals should be stated in positive rather than negative terms. The importance of a positive, optimistic approach in creating your future cannot be overemphasized. This does not mean that you should concentrate on daydreams that you do not plan to act on, but it does mean that a positive stance is much more motivating and easier to work toward than a negative one. Consider the differences between these two goal statements:

1. *Positive:* "I will budget my income better so I can save enough to tour Europe."

2. *Negative:* "I will stop wasting my money on unnecessary expenses."

The overarching goals of human existence have been the concern of thinking people throughout history. Religious people see union with God as the goal of life; for many philosophers a life of virtue and a contribution to human betterment are the goals toward which people should strive. These abstract, long-range goals are certainly worthy of reflection; but in the activities in this workbook, you should concern yourself with concrete goals of relatively shorter range and the specific means for attaining them.

Goals and aspirations change as needs change. You can initiate the process of planned personal growth by starting where you are now, in the present. The first task is to identify and understand what your present goals are. This task involves hard work. Nebulous thoughts must be translated into concrete words and pictures that accurately reflect your inner world. Questions such as "Who am I?" need to be confronted and answered with specifics.

A concept that is useful in understanding goals is to look at yourself as a living collection of constantly changing needs or expectations (goals) moving across life's continuum. Other people also can be seen as individual collections of changing needs.

## EXAMINING YOUR BROAD LIFE GOALS

A workable starting point is the identification of some broad life goals. Many of us are not conscious of our own priorities. Bringing these goals to awareness is critically important; virtually all of our actions are directly related to efforts to accomplish life goals. Our social, work, and general life goals are deeply intertwined. If we are unaware of what our broader goals are and why we behave the way we do in given situations, we act without thinking and defeat our own purposes; if we understand our goals, we can act more consistently to accomplish them.

Some broad life goals that people frequently identify are listed in alphabetical order below. In order to clarify your personal priorities, quickly rank the items on this list from 1 (most important) to 14 (least important).

**Pin it down**

| Ranking | Goal | Definition of Goal |
|---|---|---|
| _____ | *Affection* | To obtain and share companionship and affection |
| _____ | *Duty* | To dedicate myself to what I call duty |
| _____ | *Expertness* | To become an authority |
| _____ | *Independence* | To have freedom of thought and action |
| _____ | *Leadership* | To become influential |
| _____ | *Nesting* | To have a beautiful home |
| _____ | *Parenthood* | To raise a fine family—to have heirs |
| _____ | *Pleasure* | To enjoy life—to be happy and content |
| _____ | *Power* | To have control of oneself and others |
| _____ | *Prestige* | To become well known |
| _____ | *Security* | To have a secure and stable position |
| _____ | *Self-Realization* | To optimize personal development |
| _____ | *Service* | To contribute to the satisfaction of others |
| _____ | *Wealth* | To have a great deal of money |

| Note: Share the work you just completed with your partner(s). |
|---|

Next turn to Appendix A, "3. Broad Life Goals," and compare your rankings with those of others. Finally, check your rankings against your vision statement (p. 8) to make sure that your values are consistent with your vision. Change any rankings that you want.

| Note: Share your thoughts with your partner(s). |
|---|

After you have made your comparisons and any appropriate changes, complete the following statement:

*My rankings tell me that I am* . . .

1.

2.

3.

4.

5.

| Note: Share the work you just completed with your partner(s). |
|---|

The consistent factors in this ranking of people's choices are these:

1. Almost all who have chosen to do more planning in their lives have selected self-realization as a high choice. Of course, self-realization means different things to different people.

2. After reconsideration many people report that they ranked *power* and *wealth* lower than they really wanted to because of some general social beliefs that power and money are bad. In fact, power and money are neither good nor bad but are both necessary in creating most people's futures.

## THE IMPORTANCE OF GOAL CLARITY

Sloan Wilson (1969), in his autobiographical novel *Away from It All*, gives an illustration of the importance of clear goal setting. He, his family, and his friends believed that positive changes in his health, attitude toward life, happiness, and income were the result of his clearly identifying one of his life goals and acting to accomplish it. After a number of unproductive years as a writer, boredom, financial problems, and depression, Wilson recognized a long-held desire to live on his own boat. When, after planning and acting, he realized this goal, his productivity as a writer returned and his depression ended.

Health, happiness, and income are probably the strongest reasons for striving for goal clarity. But two other issues have useful implications for day-to-day living: (1) the impact of clear goals on motivation and (2) the usefulness of clear goals in developing cooperative and constructive relationships with others.

### The Effect of Clear Goals on Motivation

The clearer our goals, the stronger our motivation to accomplish these goals. When our goals are clear, we are able to focus more energy toward their accomplishment; in this way less energy is dissipated in less-important activities. All of us can think of examples (perhaps oversimplified) of times when we really made up our minds to fix a car, sew a button, finish homework, or cut the grass, and went at it vigorously and stuck with it until the task was completed. Accomplishment takes less time when energy is focused on specific action than it does when acting without planning or motivation.

The degree to which goal clarity can influence motivation is illustrated in Figure 1. Note how the information in this figure is related to the life-planning tasks you have completed so far. Without clarity with regard to a life vision and goals, it is extremely difficult to be motivated to create a future. Those of us who lack both clarity and motivation take a *reactive* approach to life and are prepared only to react to external forces and events. The reactive stance means that goals can be achieved only by accident—a rare occurrence. Those of us whose approach is *proactive* know what we want and are motivated to get it. The proactive stance puts you in charge of your own life and enables you to act on your own choices instead of someone else's—to manipulate forces and events in such a way that you turn your personal goals into reality.

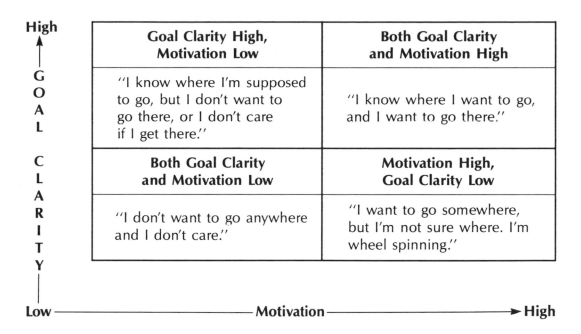

**Figure 1. Interrelations Between Goal Clarity and Motivation**

## *The Effect of Clear Goals on Relationships*

The usefulness of clear goals in developing cooperative relationships appears to conflict with what many of us have been taught about not revealing very much about ourselves. But if you have clear goals and expectations—and are willing to take some risks—you can speed up the process of working effectively with new acquaintances by talking about goals and feelings early in your relationships.

This open, proactive approach helps you to know other people faster, to build trust, to learn about their goals and to disclose your own, and to work with them to obtain mutual goals. It is important to realize, though, that this approach may deter new people if they expect a slower development of relationships. You will be sending *feelings*, and they will be expecting contact with *ideas*. Nevertheless, goal clarity allows you a choice about whether to pursue a relationship; it also allows you a higher degree of control over how quickly you attain your objective for the relationship.

## *THE ROLE OF RISK TAKING*

It may seem that taking a proactive approach to your life is fraught with risk, and indeed it is. However, as Pfeiffer (1973, p. 124)[2] says:

---

[2]From "Risk Taking" by J.W. Pfeiffer, 1973, in *The 1973 Annual Handbook for Group Facilitators* (pp. 124-126) by J.E. Jones & J.W. Pfeiffer (Eds.), San Diego, CA: University Associates. Reprinted by permission.

*It is important to understand . . . that risk is something perceived, not absolute, and that risk-taking behaviors vary greatly from society to society and among individuals within the societies. We are thrilled and awed to see the "risk" behavior of a tightrope walker whose act, in our eyes, is truly "death defying." In the performer's perception, however, his feat on the tightrope may be of little risk since he is skilled in its accomplishment; yet he may not be able to "risk" air travel, which most people easily enjoy. Challenging his supervisor may not be a risk for someone who has other job opportunities. That same challenging behavior could be perceived as a risk by a bystander who does not have other job options. Losing one's temper with a friend may be seen as an enormous risk to an individual who has been brought up to avoid conflict and as a healthy "letting off of steam" by another individual who has not been taught to suppress anger. One person's risk, then, may be another's ordinary behavior. Frequently we tend to err on the safe side, i.e., we imagine the normative boundary to be more constraining than it, in fact, is.*

Taking charge of your own life and creating your future will undoubtedly involve taking risk at some point, but several things can be done to mitigate the risk:

1. Remember that little is achieved without risk; just as a certain degree of stress is necessary to achieve anything, taking risks is necessary to grow as a person.

2. Remind yourself that it is your *perception* of an act that makes it seem risky.

3. Work on skill acquisition. After skills in particular areas have been acquired, the tasks associated with those skills seem less risky. Try to practice your skills in a safe, comfortable environment, such as that provided in a workshop or training setting, before attempting to use them in the "real" world, such as at work.

4. Let the people around you know that you are trying something new. People are generally more accepting of new behaviors if they are told in advance that those behaviors are planned and purposeful.

5. Ask for help from your family, friends, and co-workers. Ask them what ideas they have about how you can improve in particular areas of your life.

6. Remember that not making a decision is exactly the same as making a decision to do nothing differently. You cannot avoid responsibility by not making decisions.

At some point all of us are likely to find ourselves in each of the four quadrants shown in Figure 1, depending on time, interest, physical health, orientation toward risk, and other pressures and factors. Study Figure 1, determine which quadrant describes your current life goals and level of motivation, and put an asterisk in that quadrant.

---

**Note: Share the work you just completed with your partner(s).**

---

## TAKING THE FIRST STEPS

Here are some self-confronting questions: Where do I want to be at any given time? How am I going to get there? What do I have to do to get myself from where I am to where I want to be? How can I get my foot on my own accelerator pedal? What is the first small step I can take to get moving?

In the following space write the first small step that you can think of to get you where you want to go. Remember that it should be consistent with your vision statement.

---

Note: Share the work you just completed with your partner(s).

---

Turn to Appendix A, "4. Small Steps," for comparisons with what others said that their smallest steps could be.

---

Note: Share your thoughts on the examples with your partner(s).

---

After reviewing the responses in Appendix A, if you have a better idea of what your own initial steps should be, check them against your vision statement and then write them in the spaces that follow on this page and the next.

*1. My first small step is . . .*

*2. My second small step is...*

*3. My third small step is...*

## DETERMINING WHERE YOU ARE NOW

Planning and goal setting are difficult mental processes that require concentration, the right mood, and the expenditure of energy. The next task is designed to help you get into the right mood by taking a closer look at where you are now (the point in your life where you placed the check mark on your lifeline).

Before proceeding, you will need ten small pieces of paper.

On each piece of paper, write a different response to the question "Who am I?" Your framework for defining yourself may be your roles in life, your positive and negative qualities, your skills and attributes, or a combination of these. You may be able to complete this task in a very few minutes, or it may take you fifteen or twenty minutes.

After you have written your responses, spread out the ten pieces of paper in front of you. Consider each one separately, and think about what life would be like if you excluded that statement. Would you still be essentially the same person or not? In order to be more specific about this, move the sheets around until you have ranked the statements from 1 to 10. The higher-ranked statements (1, 2, and 3, for example) should be those that are most essentially you—those you could least do without. The lower-ranked statements should be those you could most easily do without. Finally, write the ten statements here, in rank order:

*My rank-ordered "Who am I?" statements:*

*1.*

2.

3.

4.

5.

6.

7.

8.

9.

10.

Now briefly note the reasons for your choices:

1. *My first "Who am I?" response is at the top of the ranking because...*

2. *The second statement is where it is because...*

3. *The third because...*

4. *The fourth because...*

5. *The fifth because...*

6. *The sixth because...*

7. *The seventh because...*

8. *The eighth because...*

9. *The ninth because...*

10. *The tenth because...*

| Note: Share the work you just completed with your partner(s). |
| --- |

Now turn to Appendix A, "5. 'Who Am I?' Statements," and compare your rankings with those of others.

---

**Note: Share your thoughts on the examples with your partner(s).**

---

After comparing, write your discoveries in the following spaces:

*I am discovering that...*

1.

2.

3.

4.



5.



After listing your discoveries, review them and decide which represents something about yourself that you are especially proud of. If none of your statements applies, write another that does. Put an asterisk by that statement.

> **Note: Share the work you just completed with your partner(s).**

Later you might want to record your statement on a 3" x 5" index card and post it or keep it where you can refer to it frequently. Life planning is hard work, and it helps to be able to remember the positive things you are learning about yourself as a result of the process. Also, you will find that concentrating on the positive is very empowering; it will renew your energies for the rest of the planning process.


## CONCLUSION

If you have completed each step to this point, you now have:

1. A linear description of your life—your lifeline;
2. A statement of your life vision;
3. Priorities for your broad life goals;
4. Three small action steps that can help you plan your life better;
5. A ranked order of statements of who you are as you presently see yourself; and
6. A list of discoveries about yourself.

This is the end of the first planning session. Put the workbook aside and wait one to four days before your next session. Reflect on the information you have accumulated about yourself; discuss it with friends or family members, and ask for their reactions.

Make a commitment to a date and time for the Second Planning Session. Record that information and today's date here:

*Today's date is* _____

*My next session will be:*

*Date* _____

*Time* _____

## REFERENCES

Pfeiffer, J.W. (1973). Risk taking. In J.E. Jones & J.W. Pfeiffer (Eds.), *The 1973 annual handbook for group facilitators* (pp. 124-126). San Diego, CA: University Associates.

Sculley, J., & Byrne, J.A. (1987). *Odyssey: Pepsi to Apple.* New York: Harper & Row.

Wilson, S. (1969). *Away from it all.* New York: G.P. Putnam's Sons.

# 4

# *Second Planning Session*

Before moving ahead, if it has been between one and four days since your last session, review your responses under the heading "Determining Where You Are Now" from the First Planning Session. If it has been more than four days since your last session, review all of your previous responses. Change any responses that you wish. This is your workbook; you may "take back," change, or add to anything that you write in it. After people have written and then thought about what they wrote, quite often they modify their thinking; that is the process of clarifying and learning.

> **Note: Share any thoughts you have with your partner(s).**

## *GUIDELINES FOR ANALYZING YOUR WORK*

The Second Planning Session provides you with an opportunity to find out more about what you like and dislike in a job. Some of the items that call for responses are not relevant for some jobs, but most will apply to whatever job you analyze. You should complete this session even if you do not think of yourself as having a job; whatever your present situation, you are engaged in some activity that you consider to be your work.

Approach this session with the same positive, proactive attitude with which you approached the last session. You may think that because you work for someone else or are subject to external pressures with regard to work, you cannot change your situation; but this is not the case. You can create your own future at work, just as you can in your personal life.

It may be true that at work certain conditions exist that limit your options. But it may also be true that you have the power to change other dissatisfying conditions. What are the sources of your power? The following kinds of work-related power have been identified by various authors (French & Raven, 1959; Hersey, Blanchard, & Natemeyer, 1979; Raven & Kruglanski, 1975).

1. *Coercive power.* This kind of power is based on the ability to induce fear. For example, if you are a supervisor, you can threaten to fire a subordinate who refuses to comply with your wishes.

2. *Connection power.* This power is based on connections with influential people either inside or outside the work place. If you are a close friend of the company president, for instance, someone may comply with your wishes in order to gain the president's favor.

3. *Expert power.* This type of power comes from expertise, skill, or knowledge. If you are particularly good at what you do or if you have some unique ability or knowledge, people may be inclined to listen to you and do what you wish.

4. *Information power.* This power results from having or being able to get valuable information. If you have this power, someone may comply with your wishes because of a desire for that information.

5. *Legitimate power.* This type of power comes with a formal position of authority in the work place. If you are a supervisor or a manager, then you automatically have legitimate power.

6. *Referent power.* This power is based on personal characteristics. If you are liked, admired, or respected because of your personality, people may do what you want.

7. *Reward power.* This kind of power comes from the ability to dispense rewards. If you can grant raises or promotions or provide people with special recognition, they may comply with your wishes in the hope that you will reward them.

Which of these kinds of power do you recognize as belonging to you?

---

**Note: Share your thoughts with your partner(s).**

---

The chances are that you have at least one kind of power. Also, if you possess a skill that is in demand in the job market, you have power in that you can probably find another job. Another point to keep in mind is that probably no one knows your specific job quite as well as you do, and your knowledge of your job gives you a certain power; no one knows better than you how to mold it to your liking and yet meet the needs of others at work.

Regardless of your power, attempting to change your job or work conditions may involve risks. Only you can determine whether those risks are worth taking. But as Block (1987, p. 11) says of striving for greatness in the work place:

> *We choose between Maintenance and Greatness.*
> *We choose between Caution and Courage.*
> *We choose between Dependency and Autonomy.*

Block suggests that striving for greatness at work—however you define it—is worthwhile even if you don't achieve it. If you don't try, it almost certainly won't happen. Three guidelines may be helpful to you as you work through this session:

1. Think of dissatisfying work conditions as *opportunities* for change rather than as *problems.* Approach them creatively; go beyond the standard alternatives.

2. If you decide to discuss certain dissatisfying work conditions with your supervisor as a result of completing this session, prepare in advance by coming up with several different *solutions* or *answers*. If you talk in terms of solutions or answers, your supervisor will be grateful to you for doing some of the work in advance, will admire your ingenuity, and probably will be more receptive to what you have to say.

3. Remember that what you want to do in your job must be in line with the mission and goals of your unit and your organization. As long as this is the case, what you want is legitimate and viable.

John Sculley (Sculley & Byrne, 1987, p. 126), says:

*A company today owes its employees one of the most rewarding experiences in their lifetimes, a chance to realize their quest to grow, to achieve, and to make a difference in the world. Nothing more, nothing less.*

## ANALYZING YOUR CURRENT JOB

It is unlikely that you are either completely satisfied or completed dissatisfied with your current job. This activity will help you clarify, analyze, and evaluate your feelings about various aspects of your job. It will also provide you with important information about your future work preferences.

*If you like your job on the whole,* it is important to identify specifically what you like about it. *If you are basically dissatisfied with your job,* analyzing your feelings will be all the more important; it may be that your dissatisfaction is with only one or two aspects that have come to assume a disproportionate, negative significance. Regardless of your attitude toward your present job, identifying the elements you like as well as those you dislike will help you plan immediate job improvements, restructuring of your present job, and/or future moves.

In this session you will develop guidelines for possible career moves in the future. You will also specify action plans for your present job that incorporate more of the elements you want and reduce those that are presently dissatisfying to you.

### Dissatisfiers

The following statements describe a number of work conditions or situations that can be dissatisfying. Read through the list and put a check mark in the blank to the left of each statement that applies to *how you feel about your current job*. Note that a few statements are incomplete so that you can fill in blanks to specify dissatisfiers. Also, at the bottom of the list you may add any other dissatisfiers that you are presently experiencing in your job. (At this point don't concern yourself with satisfiers; they will be covered in the next activity.)

_____ There is not enough variety in my work.

_____ I am not learning anything new.

_____ My boss _____ .

_____ My boss's boss _____ .

_____ My work assignments are too unstructured.

_____ My colleagues _____ .

_____ There is no opportunity to gain _____ experience.

_____ My subordinates _____ .

_____ There is not enough recognition of my contributions.

_____ My boss gives me insufficient or inappropriate feedback.

_____ There is too much time pressure.

_____ I work alone too much of the time.

_____ I work with others too much of the time.

_____ I have to write too many reports.

_____ I have to attend too many meetings.

_____ I have to make too many presentations.

_____ There is no opportunity to present, lead, be seen, etc.

_____ I have too many administrative responsibilities.

_____ I have fewer administrative responsibilities than I would like.

_____ I do not have enough autonomy in determining how I do my work.

_____ There is a lack of promotional opportunities.

_____ There is not enough responsibility to challenge me.

_____ I travel too much.

_____ I travel too little.

_____ I am poorly compensated in terms of_____ .

_____ I have to manage the budget.

_____ I have to complete these tasks that I do not like:

_____

_____

_____

_____

_____

_____ My work is physically too hard.

_____ My work does not include enough physical activity.

_____ I spend too much time inside.

_____ I spend too much time outside.

_____ _____ .

_____ _____ .

_____ _____ .

_____ _____ .

_____ _____ .

Now complete the following two items in your own words.

Hone in

1. *A short summary (a few words or sentences) of the things that are presently dissatisfying to me at work:*

*2. What I do* not *want in any job, current or future:*

---

| Note: Share the work you just completed with your partner(s). |

Turn to Appendix A, "6. Dissatisfiers at Work" and "7. Unwanted Elements in a Job," and compare your comments with those of others.

| Note: Share your thoughts on the examples with your partner(s). |

## Satisfiers

Next you will identify specific satisfiers. The following statements describe a number of work conditions or situations that can be satisfying. Read through the list and put a check mark in the blank to the left of each statement that applies to *how you feel about your current job.* At the bottom of the list add any other satisfiers that you are presently experiencing in your job.

**Pin it down**

_____ The work arrangements are flexible.

_____ The work itself is satisfying.

_____ I have an opportunity to become a supervisor.

_____ I write reports.

_____ I give presentations.

_____ My colleagues are supportive/friendly.

_____ My boss gives me appropriate feedback with an appropriate degree of frequency.

_____ My work allows me to exercise my skills in my area of expertise.

_____ My job offers me good training and development opportunities.

_____ My responsibilities are clear.

_____ I usually work as part of a team.

_____ I usually work alone.

_____ I have no one to supervise.

_____ I have the opportunity to determine for myself how I do my work.

_____ I travel to an extent that is appropriate for me.

_____ I believe in the product/service.

_____ I have the right amount of responsibility.

_____ I receive good compensation for my work.

_____ There are promotional opportunities.

_____ I have an opportunity to work with people I respect and can learn from.

_____ I have administrative responsibilities.

_____ There is a lot of variety in my work.

_____ I manage/supervise people.

_____ I am learning new things.

_____ The work is challenging.

_____ I have a reasonable amount of overtime work.

_____ I plan and set objectives.

_____ My job has high visibility.

_____ _____ .

_____ _____ .

_____ _____ .

_____ _____ .

_____ _____ .

Now complete the following two items in your own words.

1. *A short summary (a few words or sentences) of the things that are presently satisfying to me at work:*

2. *What I want in any job, current or future:*

---

**Note: Share the work you just completed with your partner(s).**

---

Next turn to Appendix A, "8. Satisfiers at Work" and "9. Wanted Elements in a Job," and compare your comments with those of others.

---

**Note: Share your thoughts on the examples with your partner(s).**

---

The last step before creating your action plan is to check your final lists of what you *do* and *do not* want in a job against your vision statement (p. 8). If there are inconsistencies, make any appropriate revisions.

## DEVISING A JOB ACTION PLAN

Now that you have identified dissatisfiers and satisfiers, put them in your own words, compared them with lists written by others, and checked them against your vision statement, you are ready to complete the following action plan. Note that you are to fill in *target dates* indicating when you will have taken the action you specify. It is extremely important to commit to completing the actions by specific dates and then to review your progress every few weeks until you have accomplished everything or you no longer feel that it is necessary to take these actions. Otherwise, you may lose sight of the goals you have set.

It is also a good idea to review your progress periodically with people who can provide objective viewpoints about your accomplishments, celebrate your successes with you, and help you with any problems you may be experiencing. You might want to consider setting up the review process on a contract basis (see Appendix B for details); some people find the formality of adhering to the terms of a contract helpful in meeting their goals.

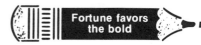

*Specific actions I will take to improve my present job:*

*1. Action:*

*Target Date:* _____

2. *Action:*

*Target Date:* _____

3. *Action:*

*Target Date:* _____

4. *Action:*

*Target Date:* _____

5. *Action:*

*Target Date:* _____

*In my next job I do* not *want to have:*

1.

2.

3.

4.

5.

*In my next job I want to have:*

1.

2.

3.

4.

5.

*Some possible jobs/assignments that match what I want:*

1.

2.

3.

4.



5.



> **Note: Share the work you just completed with your partner(s).**

Check your proposed job action plan against your vision statement (p. 8), your broad life goals (p. 10), and your "Who am I?" statements (pp. 16-17). If you find inconsistencies, make any necessary modifications.

Finally, turn to Appendix A, "10. Job Action Plans," and look at the sample responses to a similar task.

## CONCLUSION

For further work on understanding jobs that might be appropriate for you, consult a career counselor. You can find such counselors in high schools, community colleges, or universities. Many counselors are also in private practice. Another alternative is to check with your local library for:

1. A copy of *The Self-Directed Search* (Holland, 1985); or

2. The most current edition of *Dictionary of Occupational Titles* or *Occupational Outlook Handbook*, both of which are published by the U.S. Department of Labor.

You might also want to read Appendix C, which addresses the subject of career and life planning sponsored by organizations, and some of the materials listed in the Recommended Readings (see Appendix E).

This is the end of the Second Planning Session. Wait one to four days before proceeding in the workbook. In the meantime think about what you have written; discuss it with friends, family members, your supervisor, and/or your co-workers. Make a commitment to a date and time for the Third Planning Session. Record that information and today's date here:

*Today's date is* _____

*My next session will be:*

    *Date* _____

    *Time* _____

# REFERENCES

Block, P. (1987). *The empowered manager: Positive political skills at work.* San Francisco: Jossey-Bass.

French, J.R.P., Jr., & Raven, B. (1959). The bases of social power. In D. Cartwright (Ed.), *Studies in social power* (pp. 150-167). Ann Arbor, MI: Institute for Social Research, The University of Michigan.

Hersey, P., Blanchard, K.H., & Natemeyer, W.E. (1979). *Situational leadership, perception, and the impact of power.* Escondido, CA: Center for Leadership Studies.

Holland, J. (1985). *The self-directed search.* Odessa, FL: Psychological Assessment Resources.

Raven, B.H., & Kruglanski, W. (1975). Conflict and power. In P.G. Swingle (Ed.), *The structure of conflict* (pp. 177-219). New York: Academic Press.

Sculley, J., & Byrne, J.A. (1987). *Odyssey: Pepsi to Apple.* New York: Harper & Row.

**5**

# *Third Planning Session*

Before moving ahead, if it has been between one and four days since your last session, briefly review your responses under the heading "Devising a Job Action Plan" from the Second Planning Session. If it has been more than four days, review all of your responses from that session. For a complete review, skim everything you have written so far. As mentioned before, this is your workbook and you should feel free to change anything you wish.

---

**Note: Share any thoughts you have with your partner(s).**

---

## *LOOKING AT YOUR FUTURE*

This session starts by inviting you to project your thoughts into the future to a time near the end of your life. In the space provided on this page and the next, write a two- or three-paragraph autobiography consisting of some things that you would like to have said or written about you near the end of your life. Write about things that are possible, things that you might be able to accomplish; but also try to stretch yourself, thinking of the ways in which you would like to grow. For example, what might be said about you in *Who's Who* when you are very old?

*My autobiography:*

Note: Share the work you just completed with your partner(s).

Now develop a specific picture of some point in your future. Select a future time that feels comfortable to you, whether it is six months or twenty years from now. Develop a fantasy of a day that you might spend during that time period, and write your answers to the following questions:

*My fantasy day:*

*1. What is the date?*

*2. What will I be doing?*

*3. Where will I be?*

*4. Who will I be with?*

*5. How will I feel?*

| Note: Share the work you just completed with your partner(s). |
| --- |

Now refer to Appendix A, "11. Autobiographies" and "12. Days in the Future," and compare your comments with those of others.

| Note: Share your thoughts on the examples with your partner(s). |
| --- |

Next, in the space that follows, write the goals that are implied in your autobiography and your day in the future. These goals may not be absolutely clear, but they are those things you have written about that you do not now have or have not yet accomplished. If you have difficulty identifying your goals, ask someone to help you.

*Some goals implied in my autobiography and my day in the future:*

*1.*

*2.*

*3.*

*4.*

Share the work you just completed with your partner(s).

Now review your "Who am I?" statements from the First Planning Session (pp. 16-17), and in the following space add some "Who I would like to be" statements. Try not to confine your statements to safe, easily achievable things; don't exclude anything you want unless you are not really committed to working to achieve it.

Aim high

*Who I would like to be:*

1.

2.

3.

4.

5.

Note: Share the work you just completed with your partner(s).

Next compare your "Who I would like to be" statements with your vision statement (p. 8) and with your rankings of your broad life goals (p. 10), checking for consistency. If you do find consistency, you are starting to see that some clear themes are developing. If not, don't be discouraged; continue working through the workbook, and your themes should become clearer to you. Themes are bits of information about you that reappear in many of the activities you are completing. If they keep coming up, they must be important to you and they deserve your attention.

## GUIDELINES FOR PERSONAL GOALS

Some guidelines or criteria for identifying goals and making them work are listed here. These guidelines will make the task of personal goal setting more useful and satisfying.

> **Note: As you read these guidelines,**
> **share your thoughts about them with your partner(s).**

1. *Your goals must be your own.* This point has been made previously in this workbook, but it is important enough to repeat. You are more likely to accomplish personal goals that you set for yourself than you are if others set them for you. This does not mean that you cannot listen to suggestions from a spouse, friend, or supervisor and then accept the suggested goals as your own. However, your motivation and commitment will be stronger if you consciously think through—and talk through—the advantages and disadvantages of working toward a goal and then make your own decision to pursue it.

Setting your own goals is a big responsibility; it puts you in control of your life. Being in control means that you bear the responsibility for your mistakes, and it also means that you deserve the glory of your victories and successes. Knowing who you are and what you want is essential in establishing goals based on your own internalized values.

An accomplishment does not have to meet other people's needs in order to be important and gratifying. For example, some people may perceive little value in winning a prize for the best dessert at the county fair; but winning may be very important to the cook in terms of building self-esteem or progressing to future efforts. The most constructive goals for you are those that you have determined for yourself.

2. *Goals need to be clear, concrete, and written down.* The purpose of writing goals is to clarify them and make them concrete for yourself. The process of writing and revising goals also forces you to make a commitment to yourself; once a goal is written, you have a greater investment in it than before it was written. Writing helps to keep the goal in front of you and reduces the possibility that it will be forgotten as new problems and new challenges appear. Also, writing your goals enables you to integrate them into projects and to identify conflicts between or among goals. If you intend to take personal goal setting seriously, you must write down your goals and revise them continually.

3. *Start with short-range goals.* Start your goal setting by working on some short-range goals that are easily attainable. As these are accomplished, you will gain more and more confidence to tackle more challenging, long-range goals.

Short-range goals also are more likely to be within your own control. Don't be concerned if your first statement of goals is broad or unclear. But start with goals covering days, weeks, or months rather than years. In this way you will improve your probability of success. On pages 15 and 16 you were asked to write several small steps toward your own goal-setting activity. Have you accomplished them yet? If you have, how do they make you feel? If you have not accomplished them yet, either the steps you identified were too big or your commitment was too low.

4. *Consider legality, morality, and ethics in your goals.* Most people's value systems include some degree of concern with the legality, morality, and ethics of their actions. You should consider these issues before you commit yourself to a goal. It sometimes helps to answer the question "How will I feel when this goal is accomplished?" Is your goal legal in your society? If it is not, are you willing to pay the price that society imposes for accomplishing it if you are caught? Does it really fit with your moral, religious, or ethical beliefs? If it does not fit, are you willing to endure the self-inflicted guilt and the pressure imposed by others if you accomplish the goal?

5. *Goals require realism and should be attainable.* Having a goal is the first step to action; but if it is unrealistic or unattainable, it is pure fantasy and daydreaming rather than a goal. Saying that goals must be realistic does not mean that they should be low, but that *they must represent a reasonable objective toward which you are willing and able to work.* Also, there is no paradox in having goals that are both high and realistic. The higher the goal, the stronger the motivation. But if you truly do not believe that accomplishment is possible, there is probably no motivation.

The question of attainability is a troublesome one. Our society is changing so fast that predictability is difficult. Who judges attainability? Each individual has to judge it for himself or herself. If it feels right to you, and if it makes sense to you and to those you love and respect, then it is possible. Some planners now believe that if you can visualize it, you can accomplish it.

The most common hazard facing people as they begin to set goals is overambition. It feels so exciting and good to set goals that we tend to set too many for too short a period of time. A good guideline is to cut your first list of goals in half; then if you have more than six, keep paring the list until you have no more than six new goals to work on at one time.

6. *Specific time deadlines aid in accomplishment of goals.* This is another point that has been made previously and needs to be stressed again. Assigning target dates for completing each step of a plan provides constant reinforcement and a sense of accomplishment, which, in turn, help sustain your motivation. Dates can and should be adjusted with changed conditions to be more realistic, but they are an important part of setting goals. A target date should be part of any written goal.

To summarize these guidelines, the most effective goals *are self-determined, are written down, have time deadlines, are within your control, have been carefully thought through in terms of consequences, and are based on your personal values.* Goals can be revised continually to make them more realistic.

## COMPLETING A LIFE INVENTORY

This life-inventory step is a display of all the things you do and would like to do—your activities and your values. There are eight categories for you to respond to:

1. Peak Experiences I Have Had;
2. Things I Do Well;
3. Things I Do Poorly;
4. Things I Would Like to Stop Doing;
5. Things I Would Like to Learn to Do Well;
6. Values I Want to Actualize;
7. Peak Experiences I Would Like to Have; and
8. Things I Would Like to Start Doing Now.

There will be some overlap and duplication in your responses, but don't let this fact hamper you. Move quickly and spontaneously in responding; just write what first comes to mind, and don't edit what you have written.

Creative juices flowing...

## 1. Peak Experiences I Have Had

These are great moments in your life. They do not have to be the most exquisite moments you have ever had, but they should be the great times when you felt you were really living and enjoying life. Your list should include things that matter to you because they have made you feel glad that you are human and alive.

## 2. Things I Do Well

Boast about yourself and focus on your strengths. Some of the things you do well will be things that are very meaningful to you; others may simply bore you. List all that you can think of quickly.

## 3. Things I Do Poorly

These are things that you do not do well, but for some reason you want to do them or must do them. Don't list things that you have no interest in doing and do not need to do.

## 4. Things I Would Like to Stop Doing

All of us know of things that we would like to stop doing. For you, these might or might not be things that for some reason you have to do. After you complete this session, you might want to check with friends, family members, or close associates and ask them to suggest some things that they think you should stop doing.

## 5. Things I Would Like to Learn to Do Well

These are things that you must do well and things that you want to do well.

## 6. Values I Want to Actualize

These are things you want that do not fit in any of the other categories. This category may seem less clear to you than the others, but remember that many of the intangible aspects of life are values.

## 7. Peak Experiences I Would Like to Have

These are things that you would like to have happen to you. They may be new experiences or ones that you would like to have again.

## 8. Things I Would Like to Start Doing Now

List those things that come to mind as you write. Don't censor anything.

---

**Note: Share the work you just completed with your partner(s).**

---

Go back over the items listed, assign target dates to those that you definitely want to accomplish, and check those final items for consistency with the guidelines for personal goals that were discussed immediately before the life inventory. Plan to review the final items frequently. You might want to write each of the final items and its target date on a separate 3″ x 5″ card and keep or post the cards where you can refer to them often.

Now review the comparison inventories in Appendix A, "13. Life Inventories."

---

**Note: Share your thoughts on the examples with your partner(s).**

---

Next check your list of "Things I would like to start doing now" against your vision statement (p. 8) and against your priority list of broad life goals (p. 10). If the list of things you would like to start doing now is consistent with your vision and your high-priority goals, you are on target. If not, reconsider and revise as needed.

## CONCLUSION

This is the end of the Third Planning Session. Wait one to four days before proceeding in the workbook. Make a commitment to a date and time for the Fourth Planning Session; record that information and today's date here:

*Today's date is* _____

*My next session will be:*

    *Date* _____

    *Time* _____

# 6

# *Fourth Planning Session*

Before moving ahead, if it has been between one and four days since your last session, briefly review your responses under the heading "Completing a Life Inventory" from the Third Planning Session. If it has been more than four days, review all of your responses from that session. You may want to skim everything you have written in your workbook so far.

| Note: Share any thoughts you have with your partner(s). |
| --- |

During this session you will evaluate each of twenty-two areas of your life with regard to its importance to you; your present status in that area; and your potential in that area, given your current situation. You will also determine priorities so that you can direct your life-planning efforts toward those areas that would be most appropriate. Finally, you will discover which of the areas represent your values. Previously you rank ordered your broad life goals; now you will be much more specific, and by the end of this session you will be closer to developing action plans.

## *EVALUATING VARIOUS AREAS OF YOUR LIFE*

You can evaluate any area of your life with respect to these considerations:

1. *Importance.* How important is a particular area of your life in terms of its ability to bring you satisfaction? Those areas that can give you the greatest satisfaction are those that are most important to you. The more satisfaction an area holds for you, the more likely it is that you may want to do something to achieve or maintain it.

2. *Present status.* How satisfied are you with the present status of a particular area of life, with what you have achieved in that area? The poorer your achievement in a specific area (particularly one that is highly important to you), the more likely it is that you may want to do something to improve your status in that area.

---

Much of the material in this section is based on the unpublished ideas and work of Donald H. Bullock (1927-1985).

51

3. *Potential.* How much real opportunity exists in your current situation to realize the degree of satisfaction that you would like in a particular area of your life? The lower your potential for realizing satisfaction given your current situation, the more likely it is that you will have to change to a better situation or accept the fact that you may not achieve your desired level of satisfaction.

Now you are to evaluate twenty-two areas or categories of your life by rating each area from 1 to 5 on *each* of these three dimensions (its importance to you; your present status in that area; and your potential in that area, given your current situation). The rating scale is as follows:

> 1 = very important, very good, or very high
> 2 = important, good, or high
> 3 = neutral/not applicable
> 4 = unimportant, poor, or low
> 5 = very unimportant, very poor, or very low

By completing this activity, you will establish priorities for your planning efforts. The areas or categories are general, so you should *base your responses on whatever aspects of each area are meaningful to you personally.* Don't fill in the *Notes* sections until you have evaluated all twenty-two areas.

## 1. Affection (Giving and Receiving)

This area has to do with giving and receiving affection in the relationships that matter to you. Consider *physical* affection (caresses, touching, etc.), *symbolic* affection (acts of caring, gifts, etc.), and *verbal* affection (comments of an affirming, caring nature).

| Importance to Me | My Present Status | My Potential in My Current Situation |
|:---:|:---:|:---:|
| _____ | _____ | _____ |

*Notes:*

1 = very important, very good, or very high
2 = important, good, or high
3 = neutral/not applicable
4 = unimportant, poor, or low
5 = very unimportant, very poor, or very low

## 2. Appearance

This area has to do with your perception of how you appear to others in relation to how you want to appear. Consider your facial and body characteristics, your attire (clothing, jewelry, etc.), your hair, your eyeglasses or contact lenses, and so forth.

| Importance to Me | My Present Status | My Potential in My Current Situation |
|:---:|:---:|:---:|
| _____ | _____ | _____ |

*Notes:*

## 3. Art/Creativity

This category concerns your involvement, either actively (as a participant) or passively (as a spectator) in activities such as dance, music, drama, graphics (drawing, etc.), painting, sculpture, and writing.

| Importance to Me | My Present Status | My Potential in My Current Situation |
|:---:|:---:|:---:|
| _____ | _____ | _____ |

*Notes:*

1 = very important, very good, or very high
2 = important, good, or high
3 = neutral/not applicable
4 = unimportant, poor, or low
5 = very unimportant, very poor, or very low

## 4. Authenticity

This category has to do with your perception of yourself as being essentially the same person, despite the various roles you must assume in various situations.

| Importance to Me | My Present Status | My Potential in My Current Situation |
|---|---|---|
| ———— | ———— | ———— |

*Notes:*

## 5. Autonomy/Freedom

This area concerns the extent to which you control and determine your life through your own decisions, independent of constraints and restrictions. Consider your autonomy/ freedom with regard to finances, interpersonal relationships, your job, and so forth.

| Importance to Me | My Present Status | My Potential in My Current Situation |
|---|---|---|
| ———— | ———— | ———— |

*Notes:*

1 = very important, very good, or very high
2 = important, good, or high
3 = neutral/not applicable
4 = unimportant, poor, or low
5 = very unimportant, very poor, or very low

## 6. Comfort/Convenience

This area concerns your freedom from "hassles" in your everyday life. It does *not* mean your ability/willingness to confront and cope with crises and stress. Consider whether "everything has a place and is in its place," whether the people you live with or interact with frequently assume responsibilities for chores and tasks, whether you follow a general routine in your day-to-day activities, and so on.

| Importance to Me | My Present Status | My Potential in My Current Situation |
|---|---|---|
| _____ | _____ | _____ |

*Notes:*

## 7. Employment/Job/Work

This category concerns your work. Consider *career growth* (autonomy/power, positions/titles, responsibilities/roles, recognition/status), *career status* (external and internal recognition), *financial growth* (salary, bonuses/fringe benefits, profit sharing/equity), *professional skills* (administrative, client interactions, supervisory, technical), *work gratification* (challenge, clear "ground rules," rewarding relationships with co-workers, supportive environment, proper equipment), and any other issues regarding your work that come to mind. Previously you analyzed your work situation to identify specific satisfiers and dissatisfiers; now you are asked to consider your *overall* work situation.

| Importance to Me | My Present Status | My Potential in My Current Situation |
|---|---|---|
| _____ | _____ | _____ |

*Notes:*

1 = very important, very good, or very high
2 = important, good, or high
3 = neutral/not applicable
4 = unimportant, poor, or low
5 = very unimportant, very poor, or very low

## 8. Health/Physical Condition

This category concerns your general physical state. Consider *objective* issues (your medical condition and your preventive practices, your dental condition and your preventive practices, and your general physical fitness) as well as *subjective* issues (your energy; strength; vitality; freedom from irritability, fatigue, and aches and pains).

| Importance to Me | My Present Status | My Potential in My Current Situation |
|---|---|---|
| _____ | _____ | _____ |

*Notes:*

## 9. Home

This area has to do with your house, apartment, room, or wherever you live. Consider whether your home is comfortable, convenient, economical, adequate for your hobbies, adequate for day-to-day living, equipped as you need or would like, sufficiently close to work and to recreation, adequate for entertaining/socializing, and so on.

| Importance to Me | My Present Status | My Potential in My Current Situation |
|---|---|---|
| _____ | _____ | _____ |

*Notes:*

1 = very important, very good, or very high
2 = important, good, or high
3 = neutral/not applicable
4 = unimportant, poor, or low
5 = very unimportant, very poor, or very low

## 10. Hometown

This category concerns the community, town, or city where you live. Consider its characteristics and facilities: schools; housing; public services such as police, firefighters, water and sewer facilities; clean air; clean water; employment opportunities; cultural and recreational facilities; open spaces; traffic; geographical location and weather patterns; etc.

| Importance to Me | My Present Status | My Potential in My Current Situation |
| --- | --- | --- |
| _____ | _____ | _____ |

*Notes:*

## 11. Personal and Interpersonal Skills

This category has to do with your proficiency, growth, and development in both personal and interpersonal skills. Consider such skills as assertiveness, communication, openness or self-disclosure, risk taking, self-management, and so forth.

| Importance to Me | My Present Status | My Potential in My Current Situation |
| --- | --- | --- |
| _____ | _____ | _____ |

*Notes:*

1 = very important, very good, or very high
2 = important, good, or high
3 = neutral/not applicable
4 = unimportant, poor, or low
5 = very unimportant, very poor, or very low

## 12. Politics

This area has to do with your involvement in activities that are concerned with politics or social-action groups.

| Importance to Me | My Present Status | My Potential in My Current Situation |
| --- | --- | --- |
| _____ | _____ | _____ |

*Notes:*

## 13. Privacy

This category has to do with having time to yourself to read, write, think, meditate, practice yoga, or whatever you choose to do. Consider such issues as freedom from intrusions, whether you have a private place or free time, and so on.

| Importance to Me | My Present Status | My Potential in My Current Situation |
| --- | --- | --- |
| _____ | _____ | _____ |

*Notes:*

1 = very important, very good, or very high
2 = important, good, or high
3 = neutral/not applicable
4 = unimportant, poor, or low
5 = very unimportant, very poor, or very low

## 14. Recreation

This category is different from category 20, Socializing. It concerns exercising for fun (rather than for physical rejuvenation), active participation in recreational sports, vacationing, and the like.

| Importance to Me | My Present Status | My Potential in My Current Situation |
|---|---|---|
| _____ | _____ | _____ |

*Notes:*

## 15. Religious/Spiritual Needs

This area has to do with your participation in some form of worship (whatever that may mean to you) and/or whatever you do to nurture your spirit or soul (as opposed to your mind or your body).

| Importance to Me | My Present Status | My Potential in My Current Situation |
|---|---|---|
| _____ | _____ | _____ |

*Notes:*

1 = very important, very good, or very high
2 = important, good, or high
3 = neutral/not applicable
4 = unimportant, poor, or low
5 = very unimportant, very poor, or very low

## 16. Security

This area concerns your sense of well-being with respect to finances (employment, retirement, tenure in a job), your ability to care for yourself physically in the future, the stability of your interpersonal relationships, your territorial "roots" (your attachment to your home or community), and so on.

| Importance to Me | My Present Status | My Potential in My Current Situation |
| --- | --- | --- |
| _____ | _____ | _____ |

*Notes:*

## 17. Sensual Needs

This category concerns your *sensual experiences* (those having to do with the aesthetic nature of your home/work environment, massage, sauna baths, sunbathing, music, textures of clothing, etc.).

| Importance to Me | My Present Status | My Potential in My Current Situation |
| --- | --- | --- |
| _____ | _____ | _____ |

*Notes:*

1 = very important, very good, or very high
2 = important, good, or high
3 = neutral/not applicable
4 = unimportant, poor, or low
5 = very unimportant, very poor, or very low

## 18. Service

This area has to do with service of a charitable/philanthropic nature (as distinguished from such activities for the purpose of socializing). For example, it might mean work (either for pay or not) in nursing, charities, the ministry, or the like.

| Importance to Me | My Present Status | My Potential in My Current Situation |
|---|---|---|
| _____ | _____ | _____ |

*Notes:*

## 19. Sexual Needs

This category has to do with your sexual experiences. Consider such issues as frequency, quality, variety, and so forth.

| Importance to Me | My Present Status | My Potential in My Current Situation |
|---|---|---|
| _____ | _____ | _____ |

*Notes:*

1 = very important, very good, or very high
2 = important, good, or high
3 = neutral/not applicable
4 = unimportant, poor, or low
5 = very unimportant, very poor, or very low

## 20. Socializing

This area is different from category 14, Recreation. It has to do with your social life. Consider the options for interpersonal interactions that exist in your community; your opportunities to meet people; your own initiation of social interactions, given the opportunities you have; your invitations to social events; and so forth.

| Importance to Me | My Present Status | My Potential in My Current Situation |
| --- | --- | --- |
| _____ | _____ | _____ |

*Notes:*

## 21. Transportation

This category has to do with the method(s) of transportation that you typically use (for example, automobile, truck, carpool, buses or subways or other forms of public transportation, etc.). Consider the quality of your transportation, whether it meets your needs, and so on.

| Importance to Me | My Present Status | My Potential in My Current Situation |
| --- | --- | --- |
| _____ | _____ | _____ |

*Notes:*

1 = very important, very good, or very high
2 = important, good, or high
3 = neutral/not applicable
4 = unimportant, poor, or low
5 = very unimportant, very poor, or very low

## 22. Wealth/Material Possessions

This category concerns money and what it can buy. Consider those material possessions that you have as well as any that you might like to have.

| Importance to Me | My Present Status | My Potential in My Current Situation |
|---|---|---|
| _____ | _____ | _____ |

*Notes:*

After evaluating all twenty-two areas or categories, read the following guidelines for interpreting your responses:

- Areas that you rated 1 or 2 on importance and 1 or 2 on present status are areas in which you have achieved or are achieving your values; in these areas, what you want is close to what you are getting in life. It is unlikely that any of these areas will be motivational for you; you probably cannot develop high levels of new energy to expend on improving in them. By the same token, in areas in which you rated your present status as 1 or 2 and their importance to you as 4 or 5, you probably will not find the motivation to improve.

- Areas that you rated 1 or 2 on both importance and potential and 4 or 5 on your present status are potentially strong motivators for you. Although your present status in these areas is dissatisfying, they are important to you and you have a good chance of realizing satisfaction in them, given your current situation. Pay attention to them. If they are consistent with your vision statement and your broad life goals, they represent an important direction for your personal-growth efforts.

First check your responses for consistency with your vision statement (p. 8) and your broad life goals (p. 10), and jot down any notes that seem useful. Then, in the space provided on the following page, write several sentences or a brief paragraph about what you have learned from this activity.

*What I've learned about myself from this evaluation:*

---

| Note: Share the work you just completed with your partner(s). |
| --- |

If what you have just written is different from your earlier responses in this workbook, this result probably means that you are increasing your self-knowledge and are now able to be more specific and more accurate. Turn to Appendix A, "14. Insights from Evaluations," and read what other people learned about themselves after they completed similar evaluations.

| Note: Share your thoughts on the examples with your partner(s). |
| --- |

## CLARIFYING YOUR VALUES

The matrix that follows offers you a way of weighing the twenty-two areas against one another. You will be comparing the numbered categories down the left side with the lettered categories across the top. Start with the top row on the far left (Row 1) and move across the page from left to right, placing an X under each lettered column in which the category in the numbered row is currently more important to you than the one in the lettered column. For example, if *affection (giving and receiving)* is more important to you than your *appearance*, place an X in the box where Row 1 and Column B intersect; if your appearance is more important to you, leave that box blank. Also leave the box blank if the area named in the row matches the one named in the column (for example, "affection" and "affection," "appearance" and "appearance," and so on). Complete this same process for each of the twenty-two rows.

You can do it

| | A. Affection (Giving and Receiving) | B. Appearance | C. Creativity | D. Authenticity | E. Autonomy/Freedom | F. Comfort/Convenience | G. Employment/Job/Work | H. Health/Physical Condition | I. Home | J. Hometown | K. Personal and Interpersonal Skills | L. Politics | M. Privacy | N. Recreation | O. Religious/Spiritual Needs | P. Security | Q. Sensual Needs | R. Service | S. Sexual Needs | T. Socializing | U. Transportation | V. Wealth/Material Possessions |
|---|---|---|---|---|---|---|---|---|---|---|---|---|---|---|---|---|---|---|---|---|---|---|
| 1. Affection (Giving and Receiving) | | | | | | | | | | | | | | | | | | | | | | |
| 2. Appearance | | | | | | | | | | | | | | | | | | | | | | |
| 3. Art/Creativity | | | | | | | | | | | | | | | | | | | | | | |
| 4. Authenticity | | | | | | | | | | | | | | | | | | | | | | |
| 5. Autonomy/Freedom | | | | | | | | | | | | | | | | | | | | | | |
| 6. Comfort/Convenience | | | | | | | | | | | | | | | | | | | | | | |
| 7. Employment/Job/Work | | | | | | | | | | | | | | | | | | | | | | |
| 8. Health/Physical Condition | | | | | | | | | | | | | | | | | | | | | | |
| 9. Home | | | | | | | | | | | | | | | | | | | | | | |
| 10. Hometown | | | | | | | | | | | | | | | | | | | | | | |
| 11. Personal and Interpersonal Skills | | | | | | | | | | | | | | | | | | | | | | |
| 12. Politics | | | | | | | | | | | | | | | | | | | | | | |
| 13. Privacy | | | | | | | | | | | | | | | | | | | | | | |
| 14. Recreation | | | | | | | | | | | | | | | | | | | | | | |
| 15. Religious/Spiritual Needs | | | | | | | | | | | | | | | | | | | | | | |
| 16. Security | | | | | | | | | | | | | | | | | | | | | | |
| 17. Sensual Needs | | | | | | | | | | | | | | | | | | | | | | |
| 18. Service | | | | | | | | | | | | | | | | | | | | | | |
| 19. Sexual Needs | | | | | | | | | | | | | | | | | | | | | | |
| 20. Socializing | | | | | | | | | | | | | | | | | | | | | | |
| 21. Transportation | | | | | | | | | | | | | | | | | | | | | | |
| 22. Wealth/Material Possessions | | | | | | | | | | | | | | | | | | | | | | |

The numbered rows with the highest number of X's represent areas that have a high priority for you and are probably your most significant *values*. Check your values for consistency with your vision statement (p. 8) and your broad life goals (p. 10). Then use the space that follows to write several sentences or a brief paragraph on what you have learned about your values, concentrating on what you've discovered that is particularly gratifying, empowering, and motivating to you.

*What I've learned about my values:*

---

| Note: Share the work you just completed with your partner(s). |
|---|

Now turn to Appendix A, "15. Insights About Values," and read what others have learned by completing a similar activity.

| Note: Share your thoughts on the examples with your partner(s). |
|---|

## CONCLUSION

This is the end of the Fourth Planning Session. Wait one to four days before proceeding in the workbook. In the meantime, you might want to discuss your values with friends or family members and receive their input. By now you probably are acquiring a strong sense of yourself and your direction in life. Remember to celebrate your new knowledge and to congratulate yourself for having the tenacity to stick with this life-planning process. Creating a future is something that many people never take the time and effort to do; but you have taken the time and the effort, and now you are beginning to reap the rewards.

> **Note: Share your thoughts about your accomplishment with your partner(s).**

Make a commitment to a date and time for the Fifth Planning Session. Record that information and today's date here:

*Today's date is* _____

*My next session will be:*

    *Date* _____

    *Time* _____

# Fifth Planning Session

Before proceeding, if it has been between one and four days since your last session, briefly review your responses under the heading "Clarifying Your Values" from the Fourth Planning Session. If it has been more than four days since your last session, review all of your responses from that session. For a thorough refresher, quickly skim everything you have written in your workbook.

---

**Note: Share any thoughts you have with your partner(s).**

---

## GUIDELINES FOR ATTAINING GOALS

Here are seven guidelines that are useful in sustaining your momentum while working on goals. By following these guidelines, you will increase your chances of attaining your goals.

---

**Note: As you read these guidelines,
share your thoughts about them with your partner(s).**

---

1. *Combine goals into projects.* Start thinking of ways to accomplish more than one goal with the same—or only a little greater—expenditure of energy.

For example, a list of separate goals might look like this:

- Spend more time talking to the family this year;
- Take a trip to New York this summer;
- Learn more about oil painting this year;
- Get a part-time job to earn $500 by Christmas;
- Write a will in April;
- Learn to drive a motorcycle by joining the local motorcycle club next month;

- Get a hearing aid for Grandma for her next birthday;
- Get more rest at least five nights a week; and
- Improve production 10 percent this year.

Instead of working on separate strategies like these, think in terms of projects that combine several goals. For instance, planning a trip to New York with the family could help fulfill the first three goals of talking to the family, visiting New York, and learning more about oil painting. Also, it might be possible to combine motorcycle riding with earning the $500 by making money delivering things. Combining goals to form projects aids in keeping track of separate goals and in working on more than one goal at a time.

2. *Join with someone to work on mutual goals.* The example of fulfilling several goals by taking a trip to New York with the family also demonstrates the support and mutual encouragement provided by working with others on joint or similar goals. Many people have found help in getting more exercise, doing more writing, solving job problems, and improving family relationships by identifying mutual goals and agreeing to work together on them. People tend to spur one another on. Our society provides many built-in opportunities to do this through social clubs, political parties, community organizations, Weight Watchers, golf tournaments, Toastmaster clubs, bowling leagues, and so forth. If these associations do not fit your needs, it is easy to join with another person or two and start your own.

One approach that has been mentioned earlier in this workbook is to develop a written contract with another person. In such a contract you specify what you will do, by when, and so forth (see Appendix B for details). The person with whom you contract can provide assistance, encouragement, or whatever you need to keep going until you fulfill the terms of the contract.

3. *Tell people what you're trying to accomplish.* The principle behind this practice is that when one person takes a position, others with like positions or who want to support that person will gather around him or her. The effect is similar to that of joining with someone to work on mutual goals. This phenomenon is seen clearly with people who collect things. All of us know people who collect stamps, coins, thimbles, and so forth. When others find out that someone collects a certain item, they talk about this collectible with that person, give that person gifts of the collectible, and so on. This technique works with just about anything. Try announcing your goals, and others will gather around you and support those goals.

4. *Visualize a goal as accomplished.* The skill of visualization (mentally seeing something in vivid detail) is a means of bridging the gap between "what is" and "what can be." The clearer the mental picture of a goal, the easier it is to accomplish that goal. This is not only because less energy is expended in false starts and unnecessary or unwanted actions, but also because the vision itself becomes motivating; if a goal becomes so real to you that you can actually see it, you are more likely to believe that you will achieve it.

Almost everyone can link the past to the present with visualization. But to project into the future sometimes requires developing added skills in imagination, concentration, and creativity. Because all people have the capacity to imagine, concentrate, and create, all people can learn to visualize future goals more clearly. Procedures and techniques for visualizing have been articulated by Lippitt (1973). Visualization takes conscious effort and is the first step in action toward a predetermined goal. It is one way of taking a proactive stance toward your future, of creating it to your own personal specifications. The next step is making the decision to act.

5. *List the aids and obstacles to accomplishing your goal.* After you have initiated a project, the next step is to analyze the forces that might drive you toward your goal as well as those that might restrain you from your goal. Force-field analysis (Lewin, 1951) is a useful tool during this stage. It provides a way to isolate both driving (helpful) and restraining (hindering) forces, to determine the strength of each force, and to choose the forces that you have the most control over and can start action on.

Figure 2 offers an example of a force-field analysis for the goal of losing weight.[3] The line down the middle of the figure represents the goal; on the left side are listed all of the forces driving toward the goal, and on the right are listed all of the forces restraining from the goal. An arrow has been drawn next to each force indicating the relative strength of that force (a value from 1 to 5).

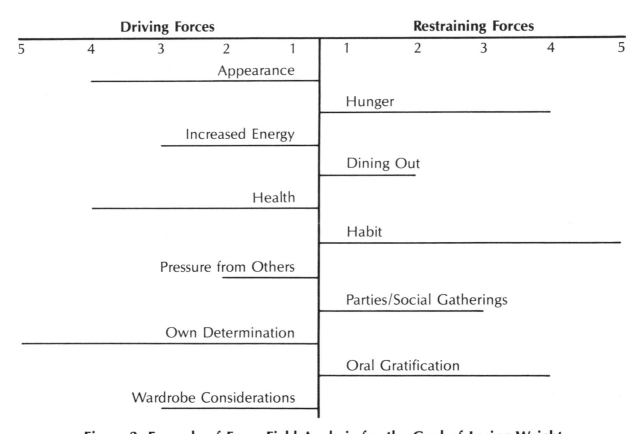

**Figure 2. Example of Force-Field Analysis for the Goal of Losing Weight**

[3]The explanation of force-field analysis that follows is from *Solutions: A Guide to Better Problem Solving* (pp. 115-117) by S.R. Phillips and W.H. Bergquist, 1987, San Diego, California: University Associates. Copyright 1987 by University Associates. Adapted by permission.

When you complete an analysis like this one, the result will be one of three situations: (1) The driving forces will outweigh the restraining forces; (2) the restraining forces will outweigh the driving forces; or (3) the two sets of forces will be about equal. If the driving forces are stronger, you can go ahead with your plans because the analysis indicates that you can reach your goal. However, if the restraining forces win out, either you will have to be extremely patient while working on your goal or you should reassess your objective. The strong forces that will be working against you may make the goal impossible to reach. In this case you may want to figure out a smaller but more realistic piece of the goal to strive for, at least at present.

If the driving and restraining forces are about equal, you may find yourself wanting to push harder on the driving forces. But if you do push harder, you may discover that the restraining forces seem to be stronger than you imagined. It is a better idea to figure out which of the restraining forces can be weakened or eliminated; if you succeed in weakening or eliminating some, you will have created a positive imbalance in which the driving forces have the advantage. Then you will begin to make progress toward your goal. (A detailed format for using force-field analysis is provided in Appendix D.)

6. *Develop visual and written supports for your goals.* The use of affirmations is commonplace. The Pledge of Allegiance, the Boy Scout Oath and the Girl Scout Oath, and songs such as "We Shall Overcome" and "Anchors Aweigh" are examples. Many different kinds of support can sustain motivation: drawing pictures or plans of your goals; writing statements; as mentioned before in this workbook, writing a brief form of the goal on a 3" x 5" card and keeping it where you can refer to it often; cutting out photos of people you want to be like or tangible items you want. For example, if there is a particular house you want to buy, take a photograph of it, hang or display the photograph where you will see it frequently, and notice how that picture keeps motivating you to act. Then make up sayings that support your goal or project—such as "I will be able to afford that house, and I deserve to live there"—and keep repeating them to yourself. This is a way of building your self-confidence and sustaining your desire.

7. *Accept the fact that change is a slow process.* It is difficult to accept this fact, understand it, and live comfortably with it. When people try to change abruptly, they are usually frustrated. You have taken years to develop and acquire your present mental processes and habits. How can you expect to be able to change them overnight? It takes time and the use of many supports to retrain yourself to be different. It is clear, though, that the only way to become something you are not is to try consciously.

## THE FAMILY LIFE CYCLE

When you create your future, you do so in the context of your life space, which may include your job, your family, and a number of other factors. One of the major factors that affects many life goals is the changing stage of the family life cycle. If you do not have a significant other, a spouse, or a family, this section may not be appropriate for you; however, if you do, you may find it helpful to reflect on how the different stages of family life will influence your goals and ways to attain them. This concept of the family life cycle can be a helpful way to view family needs and changes.

Evelyn Millis Duvall (1962, p.9) identified the following eight stages of the family life cycle:

1. *Beginning families (married couples without children);*

2. *Childbearing families (oldest child from birth to 30 months);*

3. *Families with preschool children (oldest child 2½ to 6 years);*

4. *Families with school children (oldest child 6 to 13 years);*

5. *Families with teen-agers (oldest child 13 to 20 years);*

6. *Families as launching centers (first child gone to last child leaving home);*

7. *Families in the middle years (empty nest to retirement); and*

8. *Aging families (retirement to death of one or both spouses).*

In an intensive study conducted by the YMCA, a task force identified eight dimensions of family needs through the first five stages of Dr. Duvall's schema. These stages were most relevant to the age groups served by the YMCA. As you study Figure 3,[4] which presents the results of the YMCA's project, reconsider your future and your life goals in the context of your family life.

---

[4]From *Focus on the Family* by J.M. Hardy, 1966, New York: Association Press. Copyright 1966 by Association Press. Reprinted by permission.

| FAMILY NEEDS | Stage 1 — Married Couples Without Children | Stage 2 — Childbearing Families | Stage 3 — Families With Pre-School Children | Stage 4 — Families With School Children | Stage 5 — Families With Teenagers |
|---|---|---|---|---|---|
| 1. FINDING ADVENTURE AND RECREATION TOGETHER AND SEPARATELY | —Discovering recreational activities which both can enjoy | —Maintaining adult recreational outlets————————————————————————————→ —Providing stimulating, creative experiences appropriate to children's readiness ————————————————————————→ —Developing meaningful family adventures and leisure activities - - - - - → | | | —Elaborating family adventures with special activities for teenagers |
| 2. IMPROVING HEALTH, FITNESS AND PHYSICAL SKILLS | —Encouraging wholesome release through physical skills | —Developing healthful practices and appreciation for childbearing | —Overcoming energy depletion as pre-school parents | —Developing culturally meaningful skills | —Providing explicit health education for critical areas such as smoking, drinking, venereal disease, etc. |
| 3. RELATING TO OTHERS IN THE COMMUNITY | —Establishing ways of interacting with friends and associates | —Fitting into church and community life as a young family during a period of high mobility - - - - - - - - - - - - - →  —Tapping resources, serving needs and enjoying contacts outside the family - - - → —Finding ways to fill an absent parent's shoes (temporary or permanent) - - - - - - - - - - - - - - - →| | —Tying into the organized group life of the community for parents and for children  —Developing sensitivity and a sense of concern for social problems - - - - - - - - →  —Becoming competent both as leaders and as members of groups - - - - - - - - → | —Growing into the world as a family and as individuals |
| 4. FULFILLING MARITAL AND PARENTAL ROLES | —Coming to grips with what it means to be a man, a woman, a husband, a wife and parents-to-be —Preparing for parenthood | —Providing for the developmental needs of all family members - - - - - - - - - - - →  —Developing a philosophy of discipline and learning to set appropriate limits →  —Putting into practice basic principles of sex education - - - - - - - - - →  —Preparing for brothers and sisters - - - - - - - - - → | | | —Understanding the teenager. Providing encouragement and support in developing autonomy —Assisting teenagers in developing positive attitudes toward sex and parenthood —Providing opportunities for mothers to find new challenges in life and to develop avocational and vocational skills |

Figure 3. Dimensions of Family Need
(Family Needs Appropriate for Emphasis in YMCA Work with Families)

| FAMILY NEEDS | Stage 1<br>**Married Couples Without Children** | Stage 2<br>**Childbearing Families** | Stage 3<br>**Families With Pre-School Children** | Stage 4<br>**Families With School Children** | Stage 5<br>**Families With Teenagers** |
|---|---|---|---|---|---|
| 5. SHARING RESPONSIBILITY FOR FAMILY LIVING | —Establishing patterns of who does what and who is accountable to whom<br>—Providing for effective management of money and time – – – – – | —Re-working patterns of mutual responsibility and accountability | —Sharing responsibilities with the expanding family according to age, sex and interests | —Cooperating to get things done | —Sharing the tasks and responsibilities of family living<br>—Preparing for emancipation of children |
| | | | Parental sharing of interest in and responsibility for rearing children – – – – – – – – – – – – – – – – – – ►<br>—Guiding children from dependence through independence into interdependence – – – – – – – – – – – – – ► | | |
| 6. DEVELOPING AND MAINTAINING COMMUNICATIONS | —Establishing openness in intellectual, emotional and spiritual communication | —Developing interpersonal sensitivity; emphasizing responsiveness to each other's feelings; listening for meaning; mutual assistance in self-expression | —Elaborating patterns of communication within the family – – – – – – – ►<br>—Providing for responsible participation of all family members in decision making – – – – – – – – – – – – | | —Keeping communication open in teenage family |
| 7. DEEPENING FEELING OF ACCEPTANCE, MUTUAL RESPECT AND LOVE FOR ONE ANOTHER | —Becoming a source of security, satisfaction, support and love for each other – – – – – – – – – – ►<br>—Appreciating each other's individualized satisfactions and interests – – – – – – – – – – – – – – – – – ►<br>—Accepting conflict as a part of life and learning to live with differences – – – – – – – – – – – – – – ►<br>—Enjoying other members of the family as they grow – – – – – – – – ►<br>—Demonstrating family affection and acceptance in appropriate ways – – – – – – ►<br>—Sharing love with the new members of the family – – – – – – – – – – – ► | | | | |
| 8. INTERNALIZING LASTING VALUES WITHIN A GROWING SENSE OF IDENTITY | —Establishing a new sense of identity as a couple and as individuals | —Developing self-concepts around one's values as parents | —Helping children to trust their world and to like themselves | —Re-examining family values and encouraging self-identity of each individual | Encouraging each member to verbalize, examine and internalize values by which to guide his or her life |

**Figure 3 (continued). Dimensions of Family Need**
**(Family Needs Appropriate for Emphasis in YMCA Work with Families)**

## ANALYZING YOUR FAMILY SITUATION

After you have studied the figure, complete the following five items, which will help you analyze your family situation and re-examine some of the goals, objectives, and projects that you have identified in light of your relationship with your family. Life goals are achieved *with* others; for many of us, that includes our families.

1. *I am now involved in the following stage of the family life cycle:*

2. *I would evaluate the satisfaction of my family's needs at the present stage of the family life cycle as follows:*

|  | Excellent | Good | Fair | Poor |
|---|---|---|---|---|
| *Adventure and Recreation* | _____ | ____ | ___ | ____ |
| *Health and Physical Skills* | _____ | ____ | ___ | ____ |
| *Relating to Others* | _____ | ____ | ___ | ____ |
| *Fulfilling Roles* | _____ | ____ | ___ | ____ |
| *Shared Responsibility* | _____ | ____ | ___ | ____ |
| *Effective Communications* | _____ | ____ | ___ | ____ |
| *Respect and Love* | _____ | ____ | ___ | ____ |
| *Values and Identity* | _____ | ____ | ___ | ____ |

*Notes:*

3. *My personal life goals can coordinate better with my family's needs in the following way(s):*

4. *My plans involve more effectively meeting my family's needs in the following way(s):*

5. *I am considering the following actions to enrich my role in my family:*

## DEVELOPING A PROJECT

To get started on developing a project, go back through your workbook and copy the following information. Page numbers are provided to make this task a little easier. The first five major items—your vision statement, broad life goals, action steps, "Who I would like to be" statements, and goals from your autobiography and day in the future—will provide you with a strong foundation for your project.

*My vision statement (p. 8):*

*My three highest-priority broad life goals (p. 10):*

    *1.*

    *2.*

    *3.*

*Two of my small, beginning action steps (the ones listed on pp. 15-16 or new ones):*

   *1.*

   *2.*

*My three top statements of "Who I would like to be" (p. 41):*

   *1.*

   *2.*

   *3.*

*Three goals implied in my autobiography and my day in the future (p. 40):*

1.

2.

3.

The items in the next four lists—things you would like to learn to do well, values you want to actualize, peak experiences you would like to have, and things you would like to start doing now—are important targets that you want to shoot for.

*Things I would like to learn to do well (p. 46):*

1.

2.

3.

*Values I want to actualize (p. 47):*

1.

2.

3.

*Peak experiences I would like to have (p. 47):*

1.

2.

3.

*Things I would like to start doing now (p. 48):*

1.

2.

3.

The next two lists, lowest-priority goals and lowest-priority "Who am I?" statements, will provide you with a set of items that you can trade for the things you want.

*My three lowest-priority broad life goals (p. 10):*

1.

2.

3.

*My three lowest-priority "Who am I?" statements (p. 17):*

    *1.*

    *2.*

    *3.*

The final four lists will help you focus your project ideas.

*My top-priority criteria for my work (pp. 26-35):*

    *1.*

    *2.*

    *3.*

*My three most important values to maintain (pp. 52-66):*

1.

2.

3.

*Three high-priority values that I want to work on now (pp. 52-66):*

1.

2.

3.

*Things I would like to stop doing (p. 46):*

    1.

    2.

    3.

Give some thought to combining some of your wants into projects that allow you to accomplish several goals in one major effort. Also think about your family as you consider project options. Then turn to Appendix A, "16. Projects," and look at the examples provided.

> **Note: Share your thoughts about others' projects and your own project options with your partner(s).**

Finally, write out your first project in the following space. Don't forget to include target dates where appropriate.

*My first project:*

## *THE DECISION TO ACT*

As you have seen, taking control of your own life and creating your future involve deciding to stop doing some things and to start doing some others—and then acting on your decisions. One of the risks involved is that the new activities will not be as satisfying overall as the old ones you gave up. This frequently is a frightening experience because most people have some fear of the unknown. Old axioms, such as "A bird in the hand is worth two in the bush" and "A stitch in time saves nine" condition many of us to be cautious about dropping the tested and certain for the untested and uncertain. Here are some thoughts that may help you if you are reluctant to take that first small step.

> **Note: As you read these ideas,**
> **share your thoughts about them with your partner(s).**

- The way you are, the things you do, the ways you spend your time are not the result of some external force. At some point in your life, you made conscious or unconscious decisions that resulted in your current situation. Since you made these decisions, you have the right and the power to decide to change things.

- The decisions you made over the years were most likely sound ones when you made them; they probably gave you more positive than negative payoffs at the time. As you have grown older, probably your values or your abilities have changed, and the payoffs are not as rewarding now. If so it would be logical to give up some activities and substitute others. Professional athletes are confronted with these kinds of decisions at a fairly young age. Their abilities decline, and they must develop other skills for earning a living. Most of us are not faced with decisions that dramatic, but the decisions that we do have to make are just as emotional for us.

- A decision is seldom, if ever, made only once. You remake the decision every time you are confronted with the situation. For example, a decision to lose weight and keep it off has to be remade every time hunger is experienced.

- Making decisions involves accepting your humanity and being willing to fail more than once. If as children we had as low a tolerance for failure as we do as adults, none of us would have learned to walk. How many thousands of times does a child fail before he or she learns to walk upright alone? Try not to flagellate yourself for past decisions that you might wish you had made differently, and try not to be too fearful about future decisions; life is an experiment for each of us.

- There are usually ways to reduce the risk in a decision with a trial period, a test situation, or a pilot project—or at least by discussing it with others. You might also work on your risk-taking tendency, if it is low. (Page 14 in this workbook suggests several ways in which you can mitigate risk.)

- Most people have a lot more power than they think they do. (Pages 23-24 in this workbook describe various sources of power, and you have already identified one or more of these sources as belonging to you.)

- Few if any decisions are permanent. Even major decisions such as entering or leaving a marriage, a job, a school, or a religion have been reversed many times by many people. If, after a reasonable time, your new decision does not work out, the chances are that you can reverse or modify it.

## SUMMARY

In this workbook a personal goal has been defined as something desirable and worth working for. Achieving clarity about your goals offers benefits in self-satisfaction, motivation, and collaboration with others. Guidelines and supports that have been mentioned for setting and working on goals are as follows:

- Write goals;
- Set time deadlines;
- Consider ethics;
- Develop any necessary skills;
- Be realistic, yet optimistic;
- Combine goals into projects;
- Visualize;
- Analyze plus and minus forces; and
- Develop supports.

Rather than wish you luck in your own efforts at goal setting—because luck is a function of fate—it is more appropriate to wish you:

- Increased self-knowledge, self-confidence, and self-esteem;
- A greater capacity for creativity and innovation;
- More fun out of life;
- More constructive influence over others;
- Improved clarity of everyday thinking;
- Greater tolerance for new situations;
- A greater sense of your power to create your own future; and
- A greater capacity to become that self you truly are.

You really don't need others to wish these intangibles for you. If you are working on *your* personal goals, these things are exactly what you will be achieving for yourself; and your fate will be more in your own control. Now that you have reached the end of this workbook, congratulate yourself on a job well done and move on to creating the future that you want.

> **Note: Share your thoughts and feelings**
> **about completing this process with your partner(s).**

# REFERENCES

Duvall, E.M. (1962). *Family development.* New York: J.P. Lippincott.

Hardy, J.M. (1966). *Focus on the family.* New York: Association Press.

Lewin, K. (1951). *Field theory in social science.* New York: Harper & Row.

Lippitt, G.L. (1973). *Visualizing change: Model building and the change process.* San Diego, CA: University Associates.

Phillips, S.R., & Bergquist, W.H. (1987). *Solutions: A guide to better problem solving.* San Diego, CA: University Associates.

# Appendix A
## Samples for Comparison

In the following examples, each person is identified with a number: Person 1, Person 2, Person 3, and so on. These numbers are assigned to differentiate people's comments, but the reader should not assume that Person 1 in one set of examples is the same individual who is designated Person 1 in another set of examples.

## 1. LIFELINES

*Person 1*

*I feel I've made my contributions. From here on, it's all downhill. I expect to retire and enjoy my grandchildren.*

*Person 2*

*I'm making plans to change my career. I feel I still have time to make a contribution. I'm not through yet.*

*Person 3*

*I'm in mid-career, not moving as fast as I had hoped. I want to re-examine my objectives; my choice of career was a good one, but I'm not using my opportunities.*

*Person 4*

*I didn't grow up until I was 29. Now life gets better every year.*

*Person 5*

*Things have been terribly confused with no direction. Now I'm straightening things out and setting goals.*

*Person 6*

*Agewise, I should have checked the other end, but I'm just learning to live, and I've got a lot of living left.*

## 2. VISION STATEMENTS

*Person 1*

*I have liberty, in terms of how I spend my time and in terms of financial security. My life has a lot of variety in it. I have excellent health so I can enjoy my future fully.*

*Person 2*

*To work at a career that pays me well enough to live a "well-above-standard" life style, i.e., to have enough money to travel extensively and to buy things to pamper myself without worrying about money. To achieve career goals through continual education, i.e., a doctoral degree.*

*Person 3*

*To give substance to my vision of what man can become by (1) actualizing my potential and (2) inventing characters and events that exemplify that vision.*

*Person 4*

*I want to combine my love of horses and riding with my writing talent. I want to be a great rider. I see myself loving, being loved, and making a mark.*

*Person 5*

*I will be in a warm and loving, permanent relationship with a man. I will have written at least one good novel that I am proud of and that has received critical acclaim. I will be financially secure and able to travel anywhere I want and as often as I like. I will have a home that is beautiful, comfortable, and decorated exactly as I want.*

*Person 6*

*I will be involved, dreamlike, in a reality of daily loving to go to work, creating with others in an exciting workshop that affects and benefits millions.*

## 3. BROAD LIFE GOALS

|  | Person 1 | Person 2 | Person 3 | Person 4 | Person 5 | Person 6 |
|---|---|---|---|---|---|---|
| Affection | 5 | 1 | 1 | 2 | 3 | 9 |
| Duty | 11 | 13 | 12 | 10 | 11 | 5 |
| Expertness | 10 | 8 | 10 | 9 | 8 | 3 |
| Independence | 1 | 2 | 3 | 4 | 2 | 6 |
| Leadership | 8 | 7 | 8 | 8 | 6 | 11 |
| Parenthood | 13 | 12 | 4 | 5 | 10 | 2 |
| Pleasure | 7 | 6 | 5 | 3 | 4 | 10 |
| Power | 2 | 10 | 13 | 12 | 13 | 8 |
| Prestige | 6 | 11 | 6 | 11 | 7 | 7 |
| Security | 12 | 9 | 11 | 7 | 9 | 12 |
| Self-Realization | 3 | 3 | 2 | 1 | 1 | 4 |
| Service | 9 | 4 | 7 | 6 | 5 | 13 |
| Wealth | 4 | 5 | 9 | 13 | 12 | 1 |

An analysis of these rankings shows the wide variety of goals and values that people have and illustrates how unique each of us is.


## 4. SMALL STEPS

*Person 1*

*I can continue and take the next step in this book.*

*Person 2*

*I'll talk to my spouse about our problems as soon as I get home.*

*Person 3*

*I'll continue my diet another day.*

*Person 4*

*When I see Bill, I'll ask him how he went about changing jobs.*

*Person 5*

*Think I'll just leave things alone for a while. Life is going great right now.*

*Person 6*

*Go and apologize.*

*Person 7*

*I'll go to the library tomorrow and ask for some help in finding the information I need.*

## 5. "WHO AM I?" STATEMENTS

*Person 1*

- *Teacher*
- *Parent*
- *Consultant*
- *Writer*
- *Trainer*
- *Boss*
- *Husband*
- *Bureaucrat*
- *Subordinate*
- *Friend*

*Person 2*

- *A soul in growth*
- *A pursuer of God*
- *A yogi*
- *An explorer of the inner dream*
- *A scholar of greatness (ideas/people)*
- *A writer of helpful things*
- *A friend to many/few*
- *A valuable and valued team player*
- *A wanderer lost from family*
- *A person in rapid change*

*Person 3*

- *I like to be alone*
- *I like to be with people*
- *Gentle*
- *Weak and anxious*
- *Naive*

- *Friendly*
- *Cruel*
- *Distant*
- *Strong*
- *Sophisticated*

*Person 4*
- *Wife of a special-education teacher*
- *Mother of one son*
- *Christian; active church member*
- *Secretary in personnel department*
- *Emotional; sensitive and shy at times*
- *Friendly and understanding (sometimes to the point of letting people run over me)*
- *Choir member*
- *Active Jaycee member*
- *Nervous when speaking before groups*
- *Determined*

*Person 5*
- *Writer*
- *Editor*
- *Loving*
- *Supportive*
- *Good friend*
- *Loyal*
- *Critical*
- *Funny*
- *Moody*
- *Alone*

*Person 6*
- *Soul*
- *Devotee*
- *Lady*
- *Wife*
- *Friend*

- *Confidante*
- *Auntie*
- *Nanny*
- *Fun person*
- *Encinitan*

## 6. DISSATISFIERS AT WORK

*Person 1*

1. My schedule is so tight that I do not have time to fully utilize my creative abilities.
2. Budget considerations restrict many of my most creative ideas.
3. The lack of promotional opportunities dulls my enthusiasm for being innovative.

*Person 2*

1. I would enjoy more freedom from the clock—from having to report hours, account for forty hours a week.
2. I cannot make a difference in my income (affect it, increase it).

*Person 3*

1. I am not learning new things often enough to suit me.
2. I would like greater recognition and appreciation of my team spirit (my willingness to help with other team members' work).
3. I dislike the administrative tasks that I must perform (filling out forms, etc.).
4. I dislike taking phone calls from customers and answering their questions.
5. I don't get a chance to write often enough.

*Person 4*

1. My job has become too routine.
2. At times my boss expects too much of me.
3. At times my boss is unclear, and when I ask for more direction he becomes impatient.
4. I'm not receiving enough personal computer training to help me become more efficient in my job.
5. My physical location

*Person 5*

1. Bad air—no windows!
2. Little direction from boss

3. *Little following because of no "authority"*
4. *Boredom*
5. *Lack of skill/talent in co-workers (may be interest or enthusiasm)*
6. *Lack of money at company*
7. *Lack of money in my pocket*
8. *Lack of organization*

*Person 6*

1. *Not enough autonomy*
2. *Not enough creativity*
3. *Too much "paper pushing"*
4. *I don't do anything important.*

## 7. UNWANTED ELEMENTS IN A JOB

*Person 1*

1. *A constant flow of traffic that would prohibit periods for concentrated work*
2. *Uncooperative co-workers*
3. *Work that requires constant interaction with strangers*

*Person 2*

1. *Lack of feedback*
2. *Lack of ongoing sense (through the nature of the work itself) that I make a difference—benefit others*
3. *Routine, sameness, lack of variety*
4. *No opportunity to create, to change or impact the system, product or service, or the way things are seen and done*
5. *Low pay—the gnawing sense that if I were freelancing again I could create more income to meet needs*
6. *Someone looking over my shoulder, criticizing, nitpicking*
7. *An environment with no vision*
8. *A sense of being a faceless, job-holding pawn in an implacable, changeless system*

*Person 3*

1. *Direct contact with customers (over the phone or in person)*
2. *Inadequate opportunity to learn*

3. *Inadequate opportunity to write*

4. *Paperwork (filling out forms)*

*Person 4*

1. *I don't want to be closely supervised.*

2. *I don't want to work alone.*

3. *I don't want to do tasks that don't let me fully utilize my abilities.*

*Person 5*

1. *Boredom*

2. *No windows/no air*

3. *No enthusiasm from leaders/co-workers*

4. *No enthusiasm from me*

5. *Lack of organization*

6. *Lack of imagination*

*Person 6*

1. *Dress code*

2. *Attitude of conforming*

3. *Lack of creative opportunities*

4. *Heavy bureaucracy*

5. *Poor salary*

6. *No intellectual stimulation*

## 8. SATISFIERS AT WORK

*Person 1*

*I can be engaged in my job during work hours, then pretty much forget it outside.*

*Person 2*

1. *Office hours*

2. *Co-workers*

3. *Compensation and other benefits*

4. *Location*

5. *Variety*

6. *Use of talents and skills*

7. *Autonomy*

8. *Environment*

## Person 3

1. *I love having flexible hours.*

2. *My work gives me a feeling of accomplishment. I feel needed.*

3. *I'm good at what I do, and I'm allowed to do it my own way.*

4. *I don't have to supervise people to any great extent.*

5. *My co-workers are interesting and fun.*

## Person 4

1. *The ability to use my expertise*

2. *The opportunity to work independently*

3. *Being included in the management group, although I'm not a manager*

4. *The respect I receive from my peers*

5. *The opportunity to be open with my boss*

6. *The fact that with proper justification I can influence decisions*

## Person 5

1. *I'm left alone to do my thing, mostly.*

2. *Few restrictions*

3. *Good benefits*

4. *Friendly people*

5. *Adequate pay*

6. *Flexibility*

## Person 6

1. *Peers/people*

2. *Upcoming promotion*

3. *Knowledge that I'm getting good job experience*

4. *Casual atmosphere*

5. *Benefits*

# 9. WANTED ELEMENTS IN A JOB

*Person 1*

1. *To use my creative and problem-solving skills*
2. *To receive appropriate feedback*
3. *To receive appropriate compensation*
4. *To work in a moderate geographic climate*

*Person 2*

1. *An ongoing sense of personal worth*
2. *Feedback on the benefits of what I create*
3. *Opportunity to create artistically, to imbue products or services with artistic excellence, balance, etc.*
4. *Opportunity to impact the system, to change (expand or uplift) the way people do or perceive things*
5. *Opportunity to impact earnings through additional work/projects/ideas that benefit the company—to be compensated more as what I create earns more*
6. *Decision-making power in matters of product outcome—the nature of products, how they look, how they are positioned in the market*
7. *Growth in skills, character, and understanding*
8. *People to learn from (not just in the skills of my craft, but examples of teamwork, leadership, decision making, business know-how, etc.)*

*Person 3*

1. *Flexibility in hours*
2. *Important work that I do well and am recognized for*
3. *Autonomy*
4. *Co-workers whom I enjoy*

*Person 4*

1. *To be respected for my abilities*
2. *To get satisfaction from what I'm doing*
3. *To continue growing and learning*

*Person 5*

1. *Enthusiasm*
2. *Friendly people*
3. *Encouraging, supportive boss*
4. *Sensitivity*
5. *Openness*
6. *Creativity*
7. *Windows/air*
8. *Flexibility*

*Person 6*

1. *Flexibility*
2. *Casual atmosphere*
3. *Opportunity to be creative—to write*
4. *Some physical activity*
5. *Decent salary*
6. *Reasonable independence/autonomy*
7. *Friendly, supportive co-workers*

## 10. JOB ACTION PLANS

*Person 1*

*Ways in which I can improve my present job:*

    1. *Continue to ask for more variety and involvement in other functions in staff development*
    2. *Take more initiative to be involved in other functions besides orientations*

*In my next job I want to have:*

    1. *Flexibility*
    2. *Variety in responsibilities*
    3. *Involvement in other functions besides those in my units*
    4. *Recognition for what I do*

*In my next job I do not want to have:*

    1. *As much responsibility for orientation of new personnel*
    2. *To repeat the same things over and over*

*Person 2*

*Ways in which I can improve my present job:*

1. *Budget time better*
2. *Not take on any more responsibilities until at least one current project is complete*

*In my next job I want to have:*

1. *Opportunity to continually learn*
2. *Variety in responsibility*
3. *Research*
4. *More money!*

*In my next job I do* not *want to have:*

*More than one boss!*

*Some possible jobs/assignments that match what I want:*

*Research*

*Person 3*

*Ways in which I can improve my present job:*

1. *Spend more time in the actual, day-to-day of other departments*
2. *Take more planned time off to reduce stress*
3. *Use the tools at my disposal to see a broader view*
4. *Get outside instruction or education about areas I feel I am weak in*

*In my next job I want to have:*

1. *More concerned/responsible colleagues*
2. *A secretary directly under me as opposed to one who is shared with other people*
3. *More people like the ones I currectly have working directly for me*

*In my next job I do* not *want to have:*

*High-paid whiners as subordinates (from other departments)*

*Some possible jobs/assignments that match what I want:*

1. *A vice presidency above mine and the departments that I feel are currently less productive than mine*
2. *Supervise the total automation of a company*

*Person 4*

*Ways in which I can improve my present job:*

1. *Get more involved*
2. *Take responsibility*
3. *Learn as much as I can about the business*

*In my next job I want to have:*

1. *My work recognized and not taken for granted*
2. *Responsibility given as I grow with the company*
3. *More variety in work*

*In my next job I do not want to have:*

1. *The feeling of never being caught up*
2. *A boss who never says "thanks" or appreciates my time and efforts*
3. *A boss who is never wrong*

*Some possible jobs/assignments that match what I want:*

*Business management*


# 11. AUTOBIOGRAPHIES

### Person 1

*I was born in a family where I was the youngest daughter. I did not feel loved, nor did I receive recognition. This motivated me to complete college, enter graduate school, and receive an M.A. degree in medical laboratory work. I hope that my obituary will read that I was an outstanding medical assistant, was active in politics, and was a good mother. My biggest achievement was becoming a precinct chairman and helping to elect our candidate to Congress.*

### Person 2

*Following two years at college I went into the Army. In Vietnam I reflected on my life and decided to go into my own business when I got out. One leg was damaged in the war, but it didn't keep me from becoming the owner of a dry-cleaning shop. I now own three dry-cleaning establishments. I have a family with two children. My hobby of sailing gives me recreation. I never felt that I would achieve this much, and I owe it to my wife and my own need to achieve.*

### Person 3

*I am a man who loves people, and I am constantly surrounded by those who return my feelings. I gave up a high-paying career to become a teacher of the poor. My family all died years ago, and now all mankind has become my family.*

### Person 4

*I have been a wife, mother, and grandmother. After raising my four children, I became an artist, developed a local reputation, and I have had four showings in the last year. I have put my youngest child through college with what I earned from my paintings.*

*Person 5*

*I have been rich beyond my wildest dreams, but I have tried hard to do what was right and just. This has involved me with others in a search for important humanitarian projects, and that has been the most rewarding experience of all.*

*Person 6*

*I was one of the first women to be accepted for Air Force pilot training. I have been flying since I was 18 and studied aeronautical engineering in college. I married an Air Force Officer and have happily maintained both my marriage and my career.*

## 12. DAYS IN THE FUTURE

*Person 1*

*My day in the future would be a chance to read about basic values in our country and discover them with others. I feel that in the past I've avoided discussion with others because of my inadequate education. I would like to have time in the future to learn more.*

*Person 2*

*My day in the future would be in early retirement when I could be helping young teenagers cope with life. I'd like to make enough money so I could do this without threatening the security of my family.*

*Person 3*

*For my day in the future, I would like to be on an island or in the woods alone with a girl I could love.*

*Person 4*

*I can see a Thanksgiving Day. I'll be living in a big old house on a hill. All my family and friends will be there, and we'll have a great meal and just have a good time together.*

*Person 5*

*The day I graduate will be great. I'm going to loaf in the sun and party and have fun for at least a month afterward. I'll meet lots of new people and learn about them. I may never read or study anything again.*

*Person 6*

*My picture will be in the paper announcing the publication of my book.*

# 13. LIFE INVENTORIES

The following responses are samples from the life inventories of many people; they are not presented in any particular order or according to priority.

*Peak Experiences I Have Had*

- *Sexual memories come to mind*
- *My marriage*
- *The birth of my child*
- *Recognition as a professional*
- *Being with my kids*
- *Several great learning experiences*
- *My divorce*
- *Sailing and skiing*
- *Discovering myself*
- *My last promotion*
- *Being with loving people*
- *Finding out it was okay to be me*
- *A mystical religious experience I had once*
- *Some times in my job*

*Things I Do Well*

- *Work with people*
- *Write*
- *Make things with my hands*
- *Plan*
- *Administer*
- *Teach*
- *Paperwork*
- *Cook and keep house*
- *Make love*
- *My job*
- *Sing*
- *Build*
- *Talk*

### Things I Do Poorly

- *Speak in front of groups*
- *Write clearly*
- *Manage money*
- *Relate to influential people*
- *Take orders*
- *Be a parent*
- *Play tennis*
- *Sew*
- *Be friendly with others*
- *Say no*
- *Remember names*
- *Use time well*
- *Be intimate*

### Things I Would Like to Stop Doing

- *Eating, smoking, and drinking too much*
- *Trying too hard and burning myself out*
- *A nervous habit*
- *Seeking attention*
- *Holding back in a group*
- *Talking so much*
- *Shuffling so much paper*
- *Letting people walk over me*
- *Feeling anxious and inadequate*
- *Wasting time*
- *Living with my spouse*
- *Yelling at my family*
- *Feeling depressed*

### Things I Would Like to Learn to Do Well

- *Use words*
- *Get along with my boss*
- *Paint*

- *Organize*
- *Not take life so seriously*
- *Not shoot off my mouth so much*
- *Sail a boat*
- *Play golf*
- *Be intimate with my family*
- *Love*
- *My job*

### *Values I Want to Actualize*

- *Wealth*
- *Freedom*
- *Influence*
- *Self-acceptance*
- *Self-understanding*
- *Become a friendlier person*
- *A degree*
- *Become an author*
- *Educate my children*
- *Tune in better with people, day to day*
- *Personal integrity*
- *Good health*

### *Peak Experiences I Would Like to Have*

- *Be alone on a hill at sunset*
- *Become mayor*
- *Contribute some joy to a child*
- *Win the lottery*
- *Win an election for some office*
- *To be able to give a speech that would stop groups from hating*

### *Things I Would Like to Start Doing Now*

- *More reading*
- *Goofing off*
- *Start painting*
- *Find a mate*

- *Lose weight*
- *Stop feeling inadequate*
- *Write letters*
- *Be myself*
- *Stop smoking*
- *Shop for a new car*

## 14. INSIGHTS FROM EVALUATIONS

### Person 1

*I've learned that, in general, those things that are important to me I'm currently doing with little potential to increase the degree of that satisfaction. This means I'm very happy with myself and my life right now, but there's a potential of losing that if I don't continue to find new interests and set goals. Things definitely change in life, and I must grow and change also.*

### Person 2

*Money is important to me, in terms of both security and achieving what I'd like to do. My creative and aesthetic impulses are being squelched! Unlike Dorothy, I don't think I'll find complete happiness in this backyard.*

### Person 3

*My values have been chosen explicitly, by a process of reason, so the primary value of this evaluation has been to clarify what sort of strategy will best help me accomplish my goals (values). Specifically, ranking my goals allowed me to prioritize them clearly in terms of "grounding" values and those that are secondary and will follow naturally as a result of actualizing the basic values.*

### Person 4

*My current situation is quite consistent with my vision statement. I have one potentially strong motivator—service.*

### Person 5

*Affection, art/creativity, and security are all extremely important to me; also, they all appear in slightly different terms in my vision statement. I learned two unexpected things: (1) Comfort/convenience is much more important to me than I realized; and (2) I have greater potential in several areas than I would have thought.*

## 15. INSIGHTS ABOUT VALUES

*Person 1*

My most signficant values are (1) health/physical condition—no surprise whatsoever, (2) affection—mild surprise, (3) autonomy/freedom, and (4) comfort/convenience. Autonomy/freedom and health are mentioned specifically in my vision. Comfort/convenience could be inferred from my vision.

*Person 2*

I have spent a great deal of time integrating my value premises with my vision of man and existence as well as the specific values and goals I will pursue in life. This evaluation was useful in reaffirming and crystallizing the hierarchical form of my values.

*Person 3*

I've learned that I value myself as a person; my work environment is important to me; and my recreational needs are important. Although my vision of my future states "to live a 'well-above-standard' life style," I don't think it's to achieve material wealth—but rather to meet my recreational needs. Also, my vision statement says "to work at a career" that pays well. I don't want to just "be rich"—working is important to me so that I can feel good about myself and my accomplishments.

*Person 4*

"All you need is love," I guess. I want most to love and be loved, to be independent, to be financially secure, to have somewhere to call home, and to pursue my sport. My riding (right now) means more to me than my creativity and my work. I want to be independent, but I also need the love and support of others.

*Person 5*

I've learned that affection means more to me than anything. This pleases me because wanting to receive it means that I want to connect with other people, and wanting to give it means that by doing so I can touch the lives of others in a positive way while meeting my own needs. I am apparently not as much of a loner as I thought.

## 16. PROJECTS

*Person 1*

I am interested in art, and I've been thinking I will convert my basement into a studio and invite people in. It is small, but I really want to do it. I can get it in shape this weekend, and I know two people I want to invite. I've got to do this to fill the void I've felt since my children left.

*Person 2*

*I'm going back to school for a master's degree. I should have done it ten years ago, but it's not too late. I'm going to retire in four years, and I know now I really want to teach. I will be a better teacher and have a better chance of getting a teaching job with that degree. I am going down Monday to sign up. This will get me out of the rut I'm in.*

*Person 3*

*Now that I am divorced, I've got to build a new life, meet new people, see new things. I am taking a ski trip to Vermont over Christmas. I've always dreamed about skiing. This ties in perfectly with my growing interest in photography. I just bought a new camera this week. A friend of mine was showing me some new ideas about snow photography. I am dying to try them. This meets all my criteria for a goal—short term, measurable, freely chosen—and I am happy with it. I might even meet a new partner, but that's not essential. If it happens, great; if not, it will still be fun.*

*Person 4*

*It has finally come through to me. I have a lousy job! I can't stand it! I've been kidding myself by saying I need another job before quitting. I realize now that is nonsense. I do not need the money. If I quit now, I can spend more time with my kids, and that is one of my high-priority values. I am quitting this lousy work and am going to find a way of getting paid for working with kids—that's what I really get my kicks from.*

*Person 5*

*I'm going to work with my hands creatively and design and build a patio. It is so different from my job—working with my mind. My wife has been wanting me to hire someone to do it, but I know I can do it better. She can help with the work, and we can grow closer together by working on it. I have already started on the plans.*

*Person 6*

*Hey! I see how I can combine two of my goals—growing and maturing as a person and meeting new people—into one project by attending some personal-growth training events.*

*Person 7*

*I have decided on two major goals. One is gaining a deeper understanding of religion, and another is meeting new people. I can accomplish both of these with my project to visit a number of new churches in the next few months. I have already decided that during the next four weeks I'll visit the churches where I have acquaintances.*

*Person 8*

*I am a travel nut. Since I don't have enough money to travel all I want to, my project is to find enough people who want to go where I do to pay my way. Last year I had my way paid to Europe as a guide for a group. They loved it. It was so easy. Now I need to find people who want to go to Asia. I have never been there, but I have traveled enough to know how to help newcomers who want to go to Asia. This is great! I can hardly believe that I can make my living doing what I want to do.*

**Person 9**

*I'm going to create a middle-class community organizer's school—a la Saul Alinsky and some others. This is a much-needed thing in our society—a way to get the great middle class involved in and educated about action strategies. I know it is not smart to start with a big project like this, but I've been thinking about it for a long time. It may take me ten to fifteen years, but I am willing to try. It fulfills my needs to contribute to society—for power, for recognition, for self-esteem, and for doing what I want to do when I want to do it.*

# Appendix B

## Developing Support Contracts
## for Progress Toward Goal Achievement

Often people who engage in life- or career-planning activities become quite enthusiastic about their new insights and new plans and enter a "psychological high," inspired to pursue far-reaching resolutions. Then as they distance themselves from these planning activities and move back into their daily routines, the goals that originally generated such excitement begin to fade as more immediate problems press for attention. Six months after their planning they run across the materials they completed during their planning activities and realize that they have made no progress toward their goals.

Because it is so easy to lose sight of long-range goals, it is useful to employ some mechanism for maintaining commitment to them. One such mechanism is a "support contract" developed between the individual with a particular goal and at least one other person who shares that goal. Two or more couples can also establish a contract, and so can several members of a group. However, it is a good idea for an individual husband and wife to seek at least one other party to be involved in a contract because they can gain a great deal in terms of stimulation and fresh viewpoints contributed by another party.

The parties involved in a contract should commit to keeping in touch with each other and working with each other in some limited but regularly scheduled way. Their purpose is to help each other stay focused on their mutual goal, to follow up periodically on progress toward goal achievement, and to hold each other accountable for working toward the goal. They simultaneously support and confront each other.

Not only is it possible to experience support in the long-range pursuit of goals through a contractual relationship, but also the parties can learn a great deal by being involved collaboratively with each other and sharing the results of experiences and explorations. Two heads are better than one; in fact, they are likely to be more than twice as effective.

## SOME STEPS IN DEVELOPING SUPPORT CONTRACTS

If you are considering entering into a contract with another person to complete various aspects of a life-planning process, choose someone who you feel would be reasonably congenial and someone with whom you feel you could work easily. At some point you should check with the person you choose to see whether he or she is interested in contracting with you.

Once the parties have decided to enter into a support contract, the following steps are useful.

## Make a Real Contract

Think about the contracts you are presently committed to: the mortgage on your home, the lease on your office space, the payments on your refrigerator, your marriage, and so on. These contracts are all somewhat different from one another, and yet they have a number of things in common. Each is a commitment made between parties who want something from each other and have something to give each other. Every contract, if it is to be effective, spells out the expectations between parties in specific and clear terms. The commitment is sealed with signatures on a specific document. The contract is not an end in itself in every case, but a means by which the parties hope to strengthen their commitments toward each other.

A support contract should be taken just as seriously. It should spell out as clearly as possible what each party would like to bring to and receive from the working relationship. These expectations may differ considerably from one contracting group to another; such flexibility is entirely desirable. Once the details of the agreement have been worked out, the parties should seal their commitment to each other by using a contract form.

## Determine the Features of the Contract

When you and another person are working out a support contract, consider the following guidelines and incorporate them into the contract in some way:

1. Agree on how you will communicate with each other: in writing, at periodic meetings, or both.

2. Make some initial decision on the frequency of correspondence and/or meetings. At first you may want to correspond or meet once a month or once every two months; later you may want to reduce the frequency to quarterly or semi-annual contacts.

3. Agree to review each other's goals in detail, which includes these responsibilities:
   - Testing goals in light of all the insights that the person has developed and is developing about himself or herself;
   - Checking goals against sound goal-setting criteria; and
   - Helping to develop short-term steps by which long-term goals may be pursued.

4. Plan to check each other's progress: assessing whether short-term goals are actually being achieved, helping each other attack problems that need to be solved, and reinforcing accomplishments.

5. Assist each other in revising goals as circumstances change or as the requirements of a particular goal become more realistically understood.

6. Be realistic in your expectations of each other. For example, it is much better to plan to meet infrequently but to succeed in meeting than it is to set overambitious plans that you then fail to keep.

7. Keep your correspondence and/or meetings interesting. You may want to plan an occasional social get-together, with no particular agenda.

A support contract covers a completely voluntary project, and for that very reason it is easy to let the contractual agreements slide in favor of pressing daily concerns. The actual fact, however, is that the development of your life and career is not voluntary. The only voluntary aspect is the advance planning and preparation for this development. Once events and changes have happened, planning is no longer voluntary. Consequently, it is important that you tackle the task of long-term planning now so that you can ensure a satisfying and fulfilling life for yourself in your later years, when your options will be more limited.

# Appendix C

## Career and Life Planning Sponsored by Organizations

Today's workers (both paid and volunteer) want to actualize their own potential, and a fundamental way for modern organizations to be of service to their employees is to help them examine their life and career goals to this end. Tests and counseling services are often used for youth in career planning, but it is rare to find such a service for working adults in early career or mid-career. There are counseling clinics and individual therapy for adults, but these services are usually conducted in clinical settings where individuals seek professional counselors because of being confronted with major problems. Management will probably find it in the best interest of the organization to make available, in a noncrisis atmosphere, individual and group experiences that will assist employees in reviewing, evaluating, and examining the plans they have or might have for the remainder of their careers and lives. The key to this process is a specific action plan.

The typical definition of management's job is "getting work done through people." Another, more modern definition of the task facing organizational leaders includes the dimension of "developing people through work." Such an approach is both difficult and challenging. The planning process involved in developing a path toward life and career goals is now recognized as one way to achieve this new management philosophy.

There are several good reasons that an organization may sponsor career and personal goal planning for its employees:

1. *To demonstrate the larger social responsibility of a mature organization.* One criterion of a mature organization is that it is attuned to the larger community. An organization that shows interest in the lives of its employees is being humanistic. People do not serve institutions; institutions are developed by people to serve people.

2. *To indicate to employees that the organization cares about them as individuals.* The impersonal nature of the modern organization has often been demonstrated by its acts or uncovered through research. One way for an organization to demonstrate that it is not just a machine is to show its concern for the life plans of its employees. Contrary to what many people often assume to be the case, employees who attend organization-sponsored career-/life-planning workshops are more likely to stay with the organization than to seek employment elsewhere. Enlightened managers use this kind of planning to keep their most talented people.

3. *To release the potential of the individual in behalf of the organization.* People feel more excited about their work if they see how it can help them achieve some of their life goals. The goal-planning process can help individuals see how their work experience can improve their skills, broaden their success experiences, and achieve some currently remote life goals.

4. *To help individuals prepare for change in society, the organization, and themselves.* As certain jobs become obsolete, as career interests change, as women and minority groups take their share of promotions, and as the economy shifts from a production to a service economy, many individuals need to explore ways to develop new skills and perhaps second careers. Discovering such needs and developing such potential help the individual and the organization to cope with accelerating change.

5. *To strengthen the psychological contract between individuals and the organization.* Research indicates that all employees have a "psychological contract" with the organization. In many instances this contract is weak or wholly one sided. People may not feel loyal, committed, involved, or responsible to the employer. If, on the other hand, the organization helps individuals examine their goals as human beings, a more reciprocal relationship is likely to develop. People will feel more loyalty to, and proprietorship in, the organization.

6. *To plan more effectively the learning experiences that individuals will require to achieve their life goals.* The process of planning life and career goals will help identify for individuals and the organization the additional educational experiences that are needed to achieve new skills or unreached goals. This will be helpful in the continuing education process that is an integral part of life in our world of expanding knowledge.


## ORGANIZATIONAL-NEEDS CHECK LIST

Managers can use the following check list to see if providing life-planning activities for organizational members would be in the organization's best interest. Read each item carefully and decide if it is needed by the organization. If so, then determine if the need has a high or a low priority. Put an "H" in the blank beside each high-priority item and an "L" in the blank beside each low-priority item. If an item is not a need within the organization, don't write anything in the blank.

_____ 1. Encourage and enable members to work on personal-development projects

_____ 2. Aid executives in discovering the directions of managers' development potential

_____ 3. Assist members in more effectively reviewing their career options at times of personnel cutbacks

_____ 4. Demonstrate more concern for employees' total lives and development

_____ 5. Facilitate more employee involvement in needed personnel changes

_____ 6. Strengthen the psychological contract between the individual and the organization, thus developing more loyalty

_____ 7. Identify more of the members' community interests and provide organizational encouragement and/or support of these interests

_____ 8. Identify types of training needed for member development

_____ 9. Encourage closer correlation between members' goals and the organization's goals

_____ 10. Stimulate members toward a more goal-oriented approach to life and work

_____ 11. Improve the consulting skills in project groups

_____ 12. Teach members a planning model with transfer value to other areas of work

_____ 13. More specifically identify the human resources available within the organization

_____ 14. Provide a multilevel developmental experience with minimal hierarchical conflicts or implications

_____ 15. Facilitate a more open climate within the organization

_____ 16. Improve communication among participant personnel

_____ 17. Enable mid-career managers to assess their career positions and directions

_____ 18. Improve motivation among participant personnel

_____ 19. Stimulate employee initiative

_____ 20. Integrate new members into the organization

_____ 21. Pay attention to new-employee concerns for individual uniqueness and self-direction

_____ 22. Develop regular work teams or special project teams

_____ 23. Integrate women or minority representatives into higher levels of management

If the items marked high priority are truly organizational priorities, then three or more items checked are enough to warrant considering providing support for members who wish to engage in career/life planning.

The greatest support is provided by offering group experiences, in life- or personal-planning workshops, on company time. An inexpensive beginning would be to provide workshops on each member's own time at company expense or only token expense to the member. A minimal supporting start would be to provide a workbook such as this one to each member who is interested in life planning.

Another approach would be to set up a group learning experience under professional guidance. Many colleges and universities offer standard programs, and so does the author of this workbook. In addition, consulting organizations such as University Associates offer customized programs in life and/or career planning.

# Appendix D

## Force-Field Analysis Inventory[5]

The force-field analysis inventory, adapted from Kurt Lewin's (1951) theory of planned change, helps you make a change effort specific and concrete. Part I asks you to define the problem clearly so that another person will be able to understand it. Part II asks you to specify the forces working for and against change; typically, in addition to whatever external forces you identify, this section will include your own positive motivations as well as your reservations and resistances. Part III asks you to make a specific contract with yourself to change your behavior.

## PART I: SPECIFYING THE PROBLEM

Think about a problem that is significant to you at work or in your personal life. Respond to each item as fully as necessary so that another person can understand the problem.

*1. I understand the problem specifically to be:*

---

[5]From "Force-Field Analysis: Individual Problem Solving" in *A Handbook of Structured Experiences for Human Relations Training*, Vol. II (Rev.) (pp. 82-84), by J. W. Pfeiffer and J. E. Jones (Eds.), 1974, San Diego, CA: University Associates. Copyright 1974 by University Associates. Adapted by permission. This inventory is based on a questionnaire invented by Warren Bennis and also draws in part on material developed by Saul Eisen.

2. *The following people with whom I must deal are involved in the problem:*

   *Their roles in this problem are:*

   *They relate to me in the following manner:*

*3. I consider these other factors to be relevant to the problem:*

*4. I would choose the following aspect of the problem to be changed if it were in my power to do so:* (Choose only one aspect.)

## PART II: ANALYZING THE PROBLEM

Analyze the problem by filling in the following information:

*1. If I consider the present status of the problem as a temporary balance of opposing forces, the following would be on my list of forces driving* toward *change:* (Fill in the spaces to the right of the letters. At this point don't fill in the blanks to the left of the forces.)

_____ a.

_____ b.

_____ c.

_____ d.

_____ e.

_____ f.

_____ g.

_____ h.

2. *The following would be on my list of forces* restraining *change:* (Don't fill in the blanks yet.)

_____ a.

_____ b.

_____ c.

_____ d.

_____ e.

_____ f.

_____ g.

_____ h.

3. Go back to item 1 in this part of the inventory. Using the following scale, rate the driving forces from 1 to 5 and write each force's rating in the blank beside it.

1 = It has *almost nothing* to do with the drive toward change in the problem.
2 = It has *relatively little* to do with the drive toward change in the problem.
3 = It is of *moderate importance* in the drive toward change in the problem.
4 = It is an *important factor* in the drive toward change in the problem.
5 = It is a *major factor* in the drive toward change in the problem.

4. Go back to item 2. Using the following scale, rate the restraining forces from 1 to 5 and write each force's rating in the blank beside it.

1 = It has *almost nothing* to do with restraining change in the problem.
2 = It has *relatively little* to do with restraining change in the problem.
3 = It is of *moderate importance* in restraining change in the problem.
4 = It is an *important factor* in restraining change in the problem.
5 = It is a *major factor* in restraining change in the problem.

5. In the following chart, you are to diagram the forces driving toward change and those restraining change that you rated in items 3 and 4. First write several key words to identify each of forces a through h that are driving toward change (write in the blanks created by the slanted lines); then repeat the process for forces restraining change. Then draw an arrow from the corresponding degree of force to the status-quo line. For example, if you considered the first on your list of driving forces to be rated a 3, draw your arrow from the 3 line in the "a" column to the status-quo line.

**RESTRAINING FORCES**

**Status Quo**

**DRIVING FORCES**

## PART III: DEVISING A STRATEGY FOR CHANGE

Devise a strategy for addressing the problem by filling in the following information:

1. Select two or more restraining forces from your diagram, and use the space that follows to outline a strategy for reducing their potency.

2. Apply the following goal-setting criteria (the SPIRO Model) to your change strategy. Answer each question in the space provided.

   a. *S—Specificity:* Exactly what are you trying to accomplish?

b. *P—Performance:* What action should be taken?

c. *I—Involvement:* Who is going to do it?

d. *R—Realism:* Can it be done?

e. *O—Observability:* Can others see the action?

## REFERENCE

Lewin, K. (1951). *Field theory in social science.* New York: Harper & Row.

This workbook is a step-by-step guide to designing one's future through personal goal setting. It is set up in five separate sessions, each of which can be completed by an individual working alone, by a small group of people (spouses, family members, significant others, close friends, or co-workers) working as partners, or by participants in a workshop setting. Each session requires one to two hours for an individual working alone; two or more hours for people working as partners; and three or more hours in a workshop setting, depending on the approach taken by the trainer.

The main feature of this edition of *Creating Your Future: A Guide to Personal Goal Setting* is its emphasis on an individual's power to create his or her future according to personal wants and needs. It goes beyond life and career planning in that it stresses the proactive stance, the actual molding of the future to one's own liking. Consequently, any training program based on this workbook should have a similar emphasis and should help participants to understand that they need not simply react to events.

The separate activities that comprise the sessions are all self-explanatory and do not require any special materials. Each person interested in completing the activities needs only a copy of this workbook and a pencil. However, much of the value of the process lies in bouncing ideas off others and in giving and receiving feedback. The process presented in the workbook can be extremely valuable for people working in partnerships; but it can be an even richer experience in a workshop setting, where each participant has exposure to many different perspectives. The trainer should stress this advantage to workshop participants and should consider it when designing a workshop around the workbook activities. A mechanism for sharing ideas and the results of activities has been built into the workbook, but the trainer might want to consider some of the following alternatives for varying the workbook approach:

1. *The whip technique.* The trainer asks the participants to assemble into a circle and then introduces a sentence stem, such as "One of the most important things I need in my work is. . ." or "One thing I've learned about my values is. . ." or "While I was completing this activity, I felt. . . ." The participants are instructed to take turns, each saying the sentence stem, completing it aloud, and then clarifying or magnifying if desired.

2. *"Value" listening.* The trainer explains the principles of active listening and instructs the participants to assemble into dyads. Within each dyad the partners take turns listening to each other describe the work just completed in a given workbook activity or talk about some related aspect of creating a future. While the speaker is sharing his or her thoughts, the listener listens for the *value* of the subject or how important it is to the speaker. This level of importance becomes the subject of the listener's feedback to the speaker and an ensuing discussion between the two. For example, the listener may tell the speaker, "While you were talking, I noticed that your voice rose and you began gesturing with your hands. This seems like something that means a lot to you."

3. *Assembling subgroups.* The trainer designates different areas of the room as representing different stances or positions on a given topic. Each participant goes to the area that represents his or her stance. Then the people gathered in each area are instructed to form a group, to discuss their position, and to prepare a report on their position to be presented to the total group. An alternative is to form mixed groups whose members represent two different positions and to have them discuss the merits and drawbacks of their respective positions. Subgroups can also be assembled for the purpose of contracting: The members contract with one another to carry out certain tasks associated with future planning and then make specific arrangements for following up with one another. (See Appendix B in the workbook.)

Other methods that might be useful include:

- Guided fantasy;
- Administration of any of a number of personality-assessment instruments, particularly those that relate personality to work preferences;[1] and
- Facilitation of any of a number of structured experiences designed to promote self-disclosure, feelings awareness, questioning of assumptions, or value clarification.[2]

In addition, some of the workbook activities may be assigned as prework to be completed in advance of the formal sessions.

Creating a future requires hard thought, hard work, and continual testing and revision of ideas. While running the workshop, the trainer should keep the difficulty of the task in mind and should be prepared to help the participants in any way necessary. It is most important that the trainer use a lighthearted approach to conducting the workshop. Any workshop based on this workbook is intended as a future-planning experience for participants rather than as therapy. By keeping the workshop upbeat and moving ahead with information that comes easily to participants, the focus can stay on planning.

---

[1]See, for example, *The University Associates Instrumentation Kit*, available from University Associates, 8517 Production Avenue, San Diego, CA 92121 (phone 619-578-5900).

[2]See, for example, the University Associates *Structured Experience Kit* or the UA Series in Human Resource Development, which includes the *Annuals* (published yearly since 1972) and the *Handbooks*, Vols. I-X.

# Appendix E
## Recommended Readings

Adams, J.D. (Ed.) (1980). *Understanding and managing stress: A book of readings.* San Diego, CA: University Associates.

Adams, J.D. (1980). *Understanding and managing stress: A workbook in changing life styles.* San Diego, CA: University Associates.

Barret, J., & Williams, G. (1981). *Test your own job aptitude: Exploring your career potential.* New York: Penguin Books.

Berne, P., Dubin, J., & Muchnik, S. (1980). *You've got a great past ahead of you: How women can expand their work options.* New York: Bobbs-Merrill.

Bolles, R.N. (1988). *What color is your parachute?* Berkeley, CA: Ten Speed Press.

Buskirk, R. (1977). *Your career: How to plan it—manage it—change it* (2nd ed). Boston, MA: C.B.I. Publishing.

Byrd, R.E. (1986). *C&RT: The creatrix inventory.* San Diego, CA: University Associates.

Catalyst Staff. (1981). *Marketing yourself.* New York: Bantam.

Catalyst Staff. (1982). *When can you start? The complete job search guide for women of all ages.* New York: Macmillan.

Farell, W. (1975). *The liberated man.* New York: Bantam.

Figler, H.E. (1979). *The complete job search handbook: Presenting the skills you need to get any job and have a good time doing it* New York: Holt, Rinehart and Winston.

Ford, G., & Ford, K. (1987). *Gender impressions* (questionnaire, self-teaching guide, and trainer's manual). Bryn Mawr, PA: Organization Development & Design.

Gardner, J.W. (1963). *Self-renewal.* New York: Harper & Row.

Gibran, K. (1969). *The prophet.* New York: Alfred A. Knopf.

Glasser, W.A. (1965). *Reality therapy.* New York: Harper & Row.

Goble, F. (1971). *The third force.* New York: Pocket Books.

Gornick, V., & Moran, B.K (Eds.). (1971). *Woman in sexist society.* New York: Signet.

Harris, T.A. (1967). *I'm OK—you're OK*. New York: Harper & Row.

Heath, R. (1964). *The reasonable adventurer*. Pittsburgh, PA: University of Pittsburgh Press.

Irish, R.K. (1973). *Go hire yourself an employer*. New York: Doubleday-Anchor.

Jackson, T. (1981). *The perfect resume*. New York: Anchor.

Jackson, T., & Mayless, D. (1981). *The hidden job market for the 80's*. New York: New York Times Book Co.

Komar, J.J. (1979). *Interview game: Winning strategies for the job seeker*. Piscataway, NJ: New Century.

May, R. (1953). *Man's search for himself*. New York: Signet.

Miller, G.P. (1978). *Life choices: How to make critical decisions about your education, career, marriage, family, and life-style*. New York: Thomas Y. Crowell.

O'Neill, N., & O'Neill, G. (1974). *Shifting gears*. New York: Avon.

O'Toole, J., Scheiber, J.L., & Wood, L.C. (1981). *Working: Changes and choices*. New York: Human Sciences Press.

Payne, R. (1984). *Marketing yourself for success*. Englewood Cliffs, NJ: Prentice-Hall.

Pike, J.A. (1955). *Doing the truth*. New York: Doubleday.

Robert, M. (1982). *Managing conflict from the inside out*. San Diego, CA: Learning Concepts.

Rogers, C.R. (1961). *On becoming a person*. Boston, MA: Houghton Mifflin.

Schein, E.H. (1985). *Career anchors: Discovering your real values*. San Diego, CA: University Associates.

Shostrom, E.L. (1968). *Man the manipulator*. New York: Bantam.

Storey, W.D. (1986). *Career dimensions I: Personal planning guide*. San Diego, CA: University Associates.

Storey, W.D. (1986). *Career dimensions II: Manager's guide*. San Diego, CA: University Associates.

Toffler, A. (1970). *Future shock*. New York: Random House.